READING DETECTIVE® BEGINNING

USING HIGHER-ORDER THINKING TO IMPROVE READING COMPREHENSION

Reading Detective® products available in print, software, or eBook form.

Reading Detective® Series
• Beginning • A1 • B1 • R$_x$

Math Detective® Series
• Beginning • A1 • B1

Science Detective® Series
• Beginning • A1

World History Detective® Series
• Book 1

U.S. History Detective® Series
• Book 1 • Book 2

Written by
Cheryl Block, Carrie Beckwith,
Margaret Hockett, and David White

Pen and Ink Illustrations by
Susan Giacometti

© 2014, 2001
THE CRITICAL THINKING CO.™
www.CriticalThinking.com
Phone: 800-458-4849 • Fax: 541-756-1758
1991 Sherman Ave., Suite 200 • North Bend • OR 97459
ISBN 978-0-89455-769-9

MIX
Paper from responsible sources
FSC® C011935

TABLE OF CONTENTS

INTRODUCTION

Teacher Overview v

Lesson and Practice Activity Answers vi

Student Lesson: How to Be a Reading Detective® ix

PRETESTS

Mighty Hunter 2

Bandit 6

INFERENCE

Lesson: Drawing Conclusions and Making Inferences 10

  1. Wagons West 14

  2. Why Dogs Wag Their Tails 16

  3. Did Time Stand Still? 18

  4. An Old-Fashioned Saturday 20

  5. Teeger 22

  6. Lead On, Sacagawea. 24

  7. *The Barn* 26

  8. *Sable* 28

VOCABULARY

Lesson: Defining Vocabulary Using Context 30

  9. Frontier Women 34

10. Lizard On the Loose 36

11. George Washington Comes to Class 38

12. Desert Survivor 40

13. New World for the Old 42

14. Help Solve the Garbage Problem 44

STORY PARTS

Lesson: Story Parts 47

15. A View From Above 52

16. A Foolish Wish 54

17. First Wave 56

18. Surprise Vacation 58

19. A Puff of Smoke 60

20. Invisible Spy 62

21. *Dexter* 64

MAIN IDEA

Lesson: Identifying Main Idea and Supporting Details 67

22. Your Sense of Taste 70

23. The Wright Stuff 72

24. False Face Society 74

THEME

Lesson: Identifying Theme 76

25. A Nutty Modern Folktale 78

26. Home Away From Earth 80

27. Giant Hoax 82

28. *The Cricket in Times Square* 84

CAUSE/EFFECT

Lesson: Cause and Effect 86

29. High-Rise Doghouse 90

30. Cat and Mouse 92

31. Streetball Hero 94

32. Northern Lights 96

33. Space Chase 98

34. The Secret of Popcorn 100

35. "Tracks" From *The Stories Huey Tells* 102

PREDICTION

Lesson: Making Predictions 104

36. Missing Ring 106

37. The City Street Game 108

38. Real Pirates 110

39. Pinch, Pull, Coil 112

40. Eddy the Bully 114

41. How Lies Are Detected 116

42. *Sideways Stories From Wayside School* 118

MIXED SKILLS

43. Down the Drain 120

44. All About Ants 122

45. A Skateboarder Speaks Out 124

46. A Mystery in Time 126

47. Island Patriot 128

48. Meteors 130

49. A Long Distance Adventure 132

50. Masai Culture 134

51. *Seven Kisses in a Row* 136

52. *Chocolate Fever* 138

POSTTESTS

Grandfather's Medal 140

Track and Field 144

ANSWER KEY 147

GLOSSARY 181

LITERATURE CITATIONS 182

SAMPLE ACTIVITY FROM READING DETECTIVE® A1 183

TEACHER OVERVIEW

The purpose of this program is to enable students to use higher order thinking to develop their reading comprehension skills. The reading skills are based on reading standards and assessment tests for Grades 3 and 4.

The goal of the program is to teach students how to analyze what they read. Students answer questions based on a passage and then provide supporting evidence from the text for their answers. Each sentence is identified with a superscripted number; each paragraph has a letter. Students use these numbers and letters to cite specific sentences and paragraphs as evidence.

The purpose in asking for evidence is to:

- Encourage students to go beyond simple recall of information.
- Require students to support their answers by drawing on specific information from the passage.
- Clarify for the teacher a student's thinking about and understanding of the material.
- Require students to analyze the passage in greater depth.

Contents

Pre- and posttests are provided to offer a general assessment of students' skills before and after using the program. Two passages, one fiction and one nonfiction, are offered for each. These tests are NOT intended as a formal diagnostic tool to assess a student's reading abilities. They are simply meant to give you a general idea of your students' skills in reading comprehension. They should be used only for determining which skills and lessons to focus on.

The beginning book is divided into 7 specific skill units: inference/conclusion, vocabulary, story elements, main idea/theme, cause/effect, prediction, and mixed skills. Each unit begins with a lesson to introduce and/or review the skill. A practice activity is also included. There are 7 reading passages for each skill. The last unit combines all the skills in each story.

The book contains three types of reading passages:

- Nonfiction articles on a variety of topics in the different content areas
- Fictional stories in a variety of writing styles
- Literature excerpts from award-winning and well-known authors frequently read in schools

Each exercise provides a passage for the student to read followed by a series of questions. Most of the questions are multiple choice or short answer.

A key component in this book is discussion. Some answers include explanations which show how the evidence given supports the correct answer. These explanations can be used as a basis for discussion of students' answer choices and supporting evidence. Many of the questions (inference and prediction, for example), are open to interpretation. It is important to discuss with students how they came up with their answers and how the evidence does or does not support their answers. We give what we consider to be the best possible answer based on the evidence. If you feel a student has made a good case for a response, you can accept that answer. The key to this program is encouraging students to think about what they read in order to better understand it. The evidence that a student gives is the key to pinpointing his or her understanding of the content.

LESSON AND PRACTICE ACTIVITY ANSWERS

Drawing Conclusions and Making Inferences

Students can be taught to make good inferences without actually knowing the word "inference." In this book, most of the inference questions in the student activities do not use the term "inference." However, it is a good idea to introduce the terminology along with the concept.

PRACTICE ACTIVITY (pp. 12–13)

1. **A.** Evidence: Sentences **6, 7**

   Explanation: Mrs. Henry wanted the class to make Tacy feel welcome. When no one responded, Jasmine raised her hand.

2. **Tacy felt happy.** Evidence: Sentence **13**

   Explanation: Sentence 13 supports how Tacy felt about the invitation. Smiling is an indication of happiness. It is a better choice for evidence than sentence 14, which simply tells us she agreed to lunch.

Defining Vocabulary Using Context

LESSON ANSWERS (pp. 30–31)

3. His **disheveled** hair looked as if a bird had tried to make a nest in it.

   Answer: **messy**

   Explanation: In the sentence above, his hair is compared to a bird's nest. A bird trying to build a nest would pull the hair in all directions. His hair is probably mussed up or messy, so *disheveled* means messy.

5. "You won't get away with this!" the angry man **railed** at the children.

   Answer: **shouted**

   Explanation: The man is angry. This is supported by the exclamation mark and what he says. Since he is railing <u>at</u> the children and not talking with them, he is probably shouting at them.

PRACTICE ACTIVITY ANSWERS (pp. 32–33)

1. **A**

2. **C** Evidence: Sentences **2, 3**

Story Parts

LESSON ANSWERS (pp. 47–49)

3. **The story takes place in ancient Egypt.**

Explanation: Sentences 7 and 8 tell us the workers are building a pyramid for the pharaoh.

4. **B**

Explanation: Based on sentences 4, 5, and 6, you could say Mrs. Chan was messy. Sentence 8 also supports sentence 6.

5. **Arthur is rude. In sentences 3, 4, and 5, he pushes other kids out of his way.**

PRACTICE ACTIVITY ANSWERS (pp. 50–51)

1. **A**

Paragraph **A**

2. **in the middle of the night**

Sentence **5**

3. **D**

4a. should she get help or go alone

4b. Choices **B, D**

Identifying Main Idea and Supporting Details

LESSON ANSWERS (pp. 67–68)

1. **Sentence 11 is the topic sentence of paragraph 3.**

Explanation: It tells us there are other differences between a spider's body and an insect's body. The rest of the paragraph describes these differences.

2. **The topic sentence is sentence 3.**

PRACTICE ACTIVITY ANSWERS (p. 69)

1. **A**

2. **Your skeleton has three important jobs.**

3. **5, 6, 7**

4. **It talks about how the skeleton supports and protects the body.**

Identifying Theme

LESSON ANSWERS (pp. 76–77)

What did the tortoise do that supported the theme?

He kept going. He didn't give up.

Which of the following is the best theme for the story? **D**

Cause and Effect

LESSON ANSWERS (pp. 86–88)

What were the effects of the storm?

3. [1]Trees were blown down. [2]Streets were flooded. [3]Whole houses were lifted in the air. [4]The damage was caused by a tornado that hit our town.

    Answer: Trees were blown down, streets were flooded, and houses were lifted. Sentences 1, 2, and 3 list the effects of the storm.

Cause	Effect
a strike	a safer place to work
gas ran out	had to stop
was afraid to fly	stayed home
Mother wasn't home	couldn't go outside
missed the bus	late for class

PRACTICE ACTIVITY ANSWERS (p. 89)

1. **the gorilla picked up the boy**

    signal word: **because**

2. **her face turns red, her eyes water, she gasps for air**

    Sentences **2, 3, 4**

Making Predictions

LESSON ANSWERS (p. 104)

1. **Uncle George would probably help them.**

    Explanation: Sentences 4 and 5 tell us he was always helping people. Sentence 6 says that he had never said no, so it is very likely that he would say yes.

PRACTICE ACTIVITY ANSWERS (p. 105)

Activity 1

1. **outside**

    Explanation: Sentence 2 says they always eat outside in fair weather.

Activity 2

1. **rainy**

    Explanation: Sentences 9–10 suggest that it is raining today.

2. **inside**

    Explanation: Sentences 5–8 suggest that they didn't eat outside on the days when it rained.

HOW TO BE A READING DETECTIVE®

A detective is a person who looks for clues to solve a mystery. In *Reading Detective®*, you will be the detective looking for clues, or evidence, to find the right answers.

Reading for Evidence

When you answer story questions, you may be asked for evidence. In *Reading Detective®*, evidence is the sentence or paragraph that helps you find the correct answer. Each sentence begins with a number. Each paragraph begins with a letter. When a question asks for evidence, you will write the sentence number or the paragraph letter that helped you find the right answer.

To be a good detective, you have to find the best evidence. Start by reading the story.

[1]Animals have special ways to protect themselves and to help them catch food. [2]Some animals use color to hide. [3]The polar bear's white fur matches the snow where it lives. [4]It can hunt for food without being seen.

Then read the question.

1. How can a polar bear hide when it hunts?

    _____

    _____

    _____

    Which sentence is the best evidence? _____

How did you find the answer? You looked for evidence. Go back to the story. Sentence 3 tells you that the polar bear's fur matches the snow. So the answer to question 1 is this:

The bear's white fur matches the snow.

The evidence is sentence number 3.

Sometimes the evidence is in more than one sentence and is not as direct. Read the next story.

A ¹We were playing tag. ²I was running away from Juan when I tripped and fell. ³I cut my knee on a sharp rock.

B ⁴Mrs. Jay helped me up and dried my tears. ⁵We walked to the office. ⁶The nurse cleaned the cut. ⁷Mrs. Jay hugged me and told me I was a brave girl.

Now read the question. Circle the letter of the correct answer choice.

2. What kind of person is Mrs. Jay?
   A. mean
   B. afraid
   C. kind
   D. silly

Which 2 sentences are the best evidence? ____ , ____

Go back to the story. Paragraph A doesn't talk about Mrs. Jay. Paragraph B talks about Mrs. Jay, but it doesn't tell us if Mrs. Jay is mean, afraid, kind, or silly. To answer the question, you have to look at what Mrs. Jay says and does in the paragraph.

In sentence 4, Mrs. Jay helps the girl up and dries her tears. In sentence 7, Mrs. Jay hugs the girl and tells her she is brave. Which of the four choices best describes Mrs. Jay? Mrs. Jay's actions are kind, so choice C is the best answer. There is no evidence to support the idea that Mrs. Jay is mean, afraid, or silly. Sentences 4 and 7 give the best evidence for this answer.

pretests_____

PRETEST: **Mighty Hunter** by Margaret Hockett

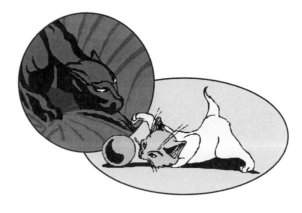

A   [1]He watches through long leaves. [2]He shifts his weight. [3]His eyes freeze on something. [4]As he stares, the thing starts to move. [5]Acting on instinct, he springs forward!

B   [6]Who is this hunter? [7]What does he hunt? [8]He is only a 4-pound kitten. [9]He catches a rubber ball that rolls by a plant in the living room.

C   [10]A young cat is lively and playful by four weeks old. [11]He is interested in anything that moves. [12]He chases things. [13]He chases his own tail! [14]Is the kitten having fun? [15]Yes. [16]He seems cute, but his play is important. [17]He is developing the skills needed to hunt. [18]He uses skills that could help him take care of himself.

D   [19]The kitten lives indoors where someone feeds him. [20]So why does he need to hunt? [21]It is his nature. [22]Besides, you never know. [23]He may have to live on his own some day. [24]Then he will use his eyes and ears. [25]He will use his balance. [26]He will use his muscles. [27]He will be able to catch his own food.

DIRECTIONS: Circle the letter next to the correct answer or write the answer on the lines given. When asked, write the number of the sentence or the letter of the paragraph that is the best evidence.

1. In sentence 3, what does the word *freeze* mean?

    A. become hard
    B. stay still
    C. become cold
    D. pop out

    Which other sentence gives the best context clue? _____

2. According to paragraph A, what causes the kitten to jump?

    _____

    Which sentence is the best evidence? _____

3. In paragraphs A and B, the action takes place:

    A. inside, in the kitchen.
    B. outside, in the jungle.
    C. inside, in the living room.
    D. outside, in the woods.

    Which sentence is the best evidence? _____

4. Kittens use their hunting skills when:

    A. playing.
    B. eating.
    C. sleeping.
    D. crying.

    Which paragraph is the best evidence? _____

5. Skitter is a 1-year-old cat. She lives indoors and is fed by her owners. Now she is outdoors and is hungry. She sees a mouse moving in the grass. Predict what she will do.

    A. nothing
    B. chase it
    C. make friends with it
    D. run away from it

    Which 2 paragraphs are the best evidence? _____, _____

6. In paragraph D, what four things help a cat to hunt?

1. _____

2. _____

3. _____

4. _____

Which 3 sentences are the best evidence? _____, _____, _____

7. The main idea of the story is that kittens' play is really:

    A. something they learn.

    B. foolishness.

    C. hunting practice.

    D. just for fun.

PRETEST: **Bandit** by Carrie Beckwith

A   [1]"No, not again!" Peter cried from the hallway.

B   [2]"What now?" Mom asked.

C   [3]"My homework is gone. [4]It was done—it was! [5]I left it on my desk. [6]Now it's gone."

D   [7]"Are you sure you finished it?" Mom asked with some doubt.

E   [8]Peter wasn't exactly a model student. [9]We were all proud when he got Cs in conduct and effort. [10]But I thought he was telling the truth. [11]Other stuff around the house was disappearing, too. [12]I couldn't find my doll, Tina. [13]One day I came home, and she was gone. [14]All that was left was her empty doll bed and a little dirt on the blanket.

F   [15]Peter rushed out the back door. [16]"I'll bet Krista threw my homework away."

G   [17]"I did no such thing!" I hollered back. [18]But Peter was convinced that he was right. [19]I followed him outside. [20]He threw off both lids and started going through the trash. [21]Bandit barked like he always did when he was excited. [22]He dug his paws into the ground, digging right alongside Peter and the trash. [23]But then Bandit stopped digging.

H   [24]"What's the matter, Bandit? [25]Did you find an old bone?" I asked. [26]I looked down the hole. [27]At the bottom was a patch of pink ruffle. [28]*Tina?* [29]Then I saw some crumpled bits of paper with Peter's handwriting. [30]It was all starting to make sense now.

DIRECTIONS: Circle the letter next to the correct answer or write the answer on the lines given. When asked, write the number of the sentence or the letter of the paragraph that is the best evidence.

1. Where did the last part of the story take place?

   _____

   _____

   _____

   _____

   Which 2 sentences from paragraph G are the best evidence? ____, ____

2. Why did Peter decide to look through the trash for his homework?

   _____

   _____

   _____

   Which sentence is the best evidence? ____

3. What do you think Krista saw inside the hole that Bandit dug?
   A. her homework and an old blanket
   B. Peter's homework and an old bone
   C. her doll and Peter's homework
   D. bits and pieces of Bandit's old bone

   Which 3 sentences are the best evidence? ____, ____, ____

4. Which of the following shows the conflict in the story?
   A. Peter is upset with the dog.
   B. Krista and Peter argue over Peter's missing homework.
   C. Mom doesn't believe that Peter finished his homework.
   D. Krista thinks Peter is stealing stuff.

   Which 2 sentences are the best evidence? ____, ____

5. Which of the following words means almost the same as *convinced* in sentence 18?

    A. wrong

    B. sure

    C. pretending

    D. lucky

6. You can tell from the story that Peter sometimes:

    A. gets As and Bs in his classes.

    B. jumps to conclusions.

    C. hides things from Krista.

    D. takes Bandit for walks.

Which 2 paragraphs are the best evidence? ____, ____

7. What do you think Peter will do if he learns that his homework is missing again?

    A. He will blame his sister Krista.

    B. He will check Krista's doll bed in her bedroom.

    C. He will go through the trash cans.

    D. He will look for covered holes in the backyard.

8. Peter did not believe his sister when she told him that she did not throw away his homework.

Which 2 sentences are the best evidence? ____, ____

DRAWING CONCLUSIONS AND MAKING INFERENCES

Drawing Conclusions

Drawing conclusions is something you do all the time. For example, Mary has to wear one of her three dresses tonight. She has a blue dress, a red dress, and an orange dress. The orange and red dresses are at the cleaners. Therefore, you can conclude she will wear the blue dress. When you read a story, you can conclude things about characters and events from the information given in the story.

Inferences and Facts

A story has two types of information, facts and inferences. Facts are clearly stated in the story. Inferences are conclusions you make based on the facts in the story. You use the facts as evidence to make your inference.

See if you can tell the difference between an inference and a fact in the following story.

1. [1]The sun glistened on the new snow. [2]Almost a foot had fallen since last night. [3]Now the sky was clear. [4]It was going to be a beautiful day. [5]"A perfect day to be sledding," thought Jorge, as his bus pulled into the school parking lot.

    Fact: There was new snow.
    Fact: The sky was clear.

    Inference: Jorge is a student.
    Inference: Jorge would rather be sledding.

The facts above are stated in the story. The inferences are decided by the reader based on the evidence in the story.

Examine the Evidence

When you make an inference, look at what really happens and what is suggested in the story. Often an author gives clues to suggest something he or she wants you to think. When you use evidence to make an inference, your inference could still be either true or false.

For instance, in the story above, the author never says that Jorge is a student riding on the bus. The inference is suggested by the words "his bus" in sentence 5. It may be true that Jorge is a student. However, it is also possible that Jorge is the bus driver.

Another example of making an inference is deciding what kind of person a character is based on what he or she says and does. You may not be told directly what this person is like, so you make a good guess based on the way he or she acts.

In the following story, what inference can you make about Sheila?

2. [1]Sheila was sitting alone at the lunch table. [2]As always, her nose was buried in a book. [3]"Is anyone sitting here?" I asked. [4]Sheila didn't answer, so I sat down. [5]"Must be a really good book," I said. [6]Sheila just sniffed and kept on reading. [7]I tried again. [8]"I like mysteries, too." [9]This time, Sheila glared at me, slammed the book shut, and left.

The paragraph doesn't state that Sheila wants to be left alone, but you could decide this from her actions. In sentence 1, she is sitting alone. In sentences 4 and 6, she ignores the narrator. Finally, she gets up and leaves. You could also decide that the narrator wanted to talk to Sheila. The narrator tries to talk to her in sentence 3 and again in sentence 7.

Using Your Own Knowledge

Sometimes when you make an inference, you use your own knowledge along with the information that is given or suggested in the text. Most people know that some snakes eat small animals. Can you use this information to make an inference about what happened to the gerbils?

3. [1]Amanda was pet sitting Alejandro's pet boa constrictor. [2]When she went to check on him in the morning, the snake was missing. [3]There also seemed to be fewer gerbils in the next cage.

It is possible that the snake and the gerbils escaped together. It is more likely that the snake escaped and ate the gerbils. In this case, the inference is probably true, but it could be false. There is not enough evidence to know for sure what really happened to the gerbils.

INFERENCE PRACTICE ACTIVITY

Read the following story. Then read the first question and circle the letter of the correct answer.

A   [1]Her eyes wouldn't leave the floor. [2]She looked scared. [3]Mrs. Henry put her arm around the girl's tiny shoulders. [4]"Students, this is Tacy. [5]She's from Austin, Texas. [6]Please try to make her feel welcome."

B   [7]No one said anything. [8]I thought someone should. [9]I raised my hand. [10]"Yes, Jasmine," Mrs. Henry asked. [11]"Did you want to say something to Tacy?"

C   [12]"Would you like to eat lunch with Lucy and me?" I asked.

D   [13]Tacy smiled. [14]"Sure," she replied. [15]Then I realized that making a friend wasn't hard. [16]It just took a little thought.

1. Why did Jasmine think she should say something?
    A. She wanted to make Tacy feel welcome.
    B. She didn't have anyone to eat lunch with.
    C. She remembered what it was like to be a new student.
    D. She saw Mrs. Henry looking at her.

To decide if you made the right choice, you need to look back at the story for evidence. What did Mrs. Henry want the class to do? How did the class respond to Mrs. Henry? How does this relate to what Jasmine did? Look at choices A and B. Which makes more sense? How about choices C and D?

You may then be asked another question like this:

Which 2 sentences are the best evidence? _____, _____

Look at paragraph A. Which sentence told you what Mrs. Henry asked the class to do? Write that sentence number on the line.

Now look at paragraph B. Sentence 8 tells you that Jasmine thought someone should say something. Which sentence in paragraph B tells you *why* she thought this?

Some questions will ask you to write an answer. Read question number 2.

2. How do you think Tacy felt after Jasmine asked her to eat lunch with her?

_____

Which sentence is the best evidence? ____

What did Tacy do after Jasmine invited her? Does that give you a clue about how Tacy felt?

Go back to the story. Which sentence tells you what Tacy did after Jasmine asked her to have lunch? Write the number of that sentence on the line.

1. **Wagons West** by Cheryl Block

[1]We had pulled the wagons into a circle for the night. [2]Families were starting their campfires for the evening meal inside the circle of wagons.

[3]Ma sent me to the river with the bucket. [4]It was dusk, and the evening was quiet. [5]As I bent to fill the bucket, I heard a rustle in the bushes. [6]As I turned to look, a large bear came lumbering out of the bushes. [7]I froze.

[8]The bear stopped and sniffed the air. [9]He looked directly at me. [10]He lowered his head and started to drink noisily. [11]I began to slowly back up when I tripped on a tree root. [12]The bucket banged loudly into a tree.

[13]The bear jerked his head up, startled. [14]I turned and ran as fast as my legs could carry me. [15]I didn't look back.

DIRECTIONS: Read each inference below. Decide if the statement is true, false, or has no evidence. Circle the correct choice. If you answer true or false, write the number of the sentence that gives the best evidence.

EXAMPLE:

Dinner will be cooked in the kitchen.

True (False)   No Evidence

Evidence: __2__

1. The child was to fill the bucket with water.

   True   False   No Evidence

   Evidence: _____, _____

2. The sun was still shining brightly.

   True   False   No Evidence

   Evidence: _____

3. The child didn't move when he first saw the bear.

   True   False   No Evidence

   Evidence: _____

4. In sentence 5, the rustle was made by the bear.

   True   False   No Evidence

   Evidence other than sentence 5: _____

5. The bear was thirsty.

   True   False   No Evidence

   Evidence: _____

6. The bear was hungry.

   True   False   No Evidence

   Evidence: _____

7. The bear was surprised by the bucket.

   True   False   No Evidence

   Evidence: _____

8. The bear chased the child.

   True   False   No Evidence

   Evidence: _____

2. Why Dogs Wag Their Tails by David White

A ¹In the early days of the animals, the dog was trying to show his happiness but did not know how. ²He decided to ask his friends for help.

B ³The dog went to the cat. ⁴"You should try purring," the cat suggested, purring.

C ⁵"You're no help," replied the dog sadly.

D ⁶The dog went to the hyena. ⁷"You should try laughing," the hyena said, laughing. ⁸"Look at me. ⁹I'm happy when I laugh."

E ¹⁰"You're no help," responded the dog sadly.

F ¹¹The dog went to the chimp. ¹²"You should try smiling," she said with a grin. ¹³The dog tried to smile. ¹⁴The chimp tried not to laugh. ¹⁵"You're right, my friend," she added. ¹⁶"I thought it would help, but you don't look happy."

G ¹⁷The dog hung his head and walked away. ¹⁸Then he had an idea. ¹⁹He would go see the lion. ²⁰The lion was wise.

H ²¹"King of the Beasts, please tell me how to look happy," the dog requested.

I ²²The lion yawned and answered, "Think of something happy."

J ²³The dog thought for a long while. ²⁴Finally, the dog thought how lucky he was to have friends like the cat, the hyena, and the chimp. ²⁵The dog's tail twitched.

K ²⁶"Aha," the lion said. ²⁷"I wondered how your happy feeling would show."

L ²⁸"I felt it!" the dog exclaimed excitedly. ²⁹The tail moved even more. ³⁰"Wow!" the dog cried. ³¹"My tail shows how happy I am! ³²Thank you, lion!"

M ³³The dog bounded off. ³⁴He couldn't wait to show his other friends! ³⁵As he ran along, his lively tail wagged after him.

DIRECTIONS: Circle the letter next to the correct answer or write the answer on the lines given. When asked, write the number of the sentence or the letter of the paragraph that is the best evidence.

1. Why did the dog tell the cat, "You're no help"?

   _____

   _____

   Which sentence is the best evidence? ____

2. Why did the hyena suggest that the dog should laugh?
   A. He wanted to make fun of the dog.
   B. Laughing made the hyena happy.
   C. Purring made the dog sound silly.
   D. He was worried about the dog.

   Which sentence is the best evidence? ____

3. What did the chimp think would happen if the dog smiled? The dog would:
   A. look happy.
   B. say he was sorry.
   C. stop looking for friends.
   D. become the chimp's friend.

   Which sentence is the best evidence? ____

4. In sentence 22, why did the lion tell the dog to think of something happy?

   _____

   _____

   _____

   Which sentence is the best evidence? ____

5. What does the last paragraph suggest about how the dog felt when he left the lion?

   _____

   _____

   Which sentence is the best evidence? ____

3. Did Time Stand Still? by Margaret Hockett

A [1]I was excited. [2]I was flying to California! [3]I started in Ohio. [4]It was 8:00 in the morning.

B [5]I had breakfast. [6]I looked at my watch. [7]We had flown for an hour. [8]The captain said it was 8:00! [9]I set my watch back. [10]"Time is slow," I thought.

C [11]I read a book. [12]I checked my watch. [13]It was two hours later. [14]Then the captain announced it was only 9:00! [15]What was going on? [16]I turned my watch back again.

D [17]I was hungry when my watch said 11:00. [18]I wondered why. [19]I usually eat lunch at 1:00. [20]The captain spoke up again. [21]"The time is now 10:00."

E [22]I figured out why time seemed so slow. [23]The United States has different time zones. [24]From east to west, each zone is one hour earlier. [25]As I traveled farther west, time got earlier!

F [26]It took me five hours to fly to California. [27]I started at 8:00 a.m. [28]But I arrived there at 10:00 a.m.!

TIME ZONES

Pacific Mountain Central Eastern

Ohio

California

WEST ⟵

EAST ⟶

DIRECTIONS: Circle the letter next to the correct answer or write the answer on the lines given. When asked, write the number of the sentence or the letter of the paragraph that is the best evidence.

1. In sentence 13, what time did the narrator probably think it was?
   A. 9:00
   B. 12:00
   C. 8:00
   D. 10:00

   Which other sentence from paragraph B is the best evidence? _____

2. In sentence 16, she probably changed her watch to what time?

   _____

   Which other sentence is the best evidence? _____

3. What if you flew from California to Ohio? For each time zone, you should set your watch:
   A. one hour earlier.
   B. one hour later.
   C. two hours later.
   D. where it already is.

   Which sentence from paragraph E is the best evidence? _____

4. In sentence 17, why was she hungry?

   _____

   _____

   _____

   Which sentence from paragraph D is the best evidence? _____

5. Altogether, the narrator was in how many time zones?

   _____

4. **An Old-Fashioned Saturday** by Margaret Hockett

A   [1]I hear a whistle and then a whinny. [2]Prancer is off! [3]I nearly fall off the edge of the sled. [4]I grab the tank for balance. [5]The sap sloshes around as we bump over rocks and glide around muddy corners. [6]The sled slows, and I jump off. [7]I trudge through ankle-deep snow.

B   [8]I'll be soaked to the skin, but what can Ma say? [9]She's the one who wanted me to go outside. [10]I didn't want to come to the woods at first. [11]Now I think it's fun!

C   [12]I take a bucket off the maple tree and carry it to the tank. [13]I pour the bucket into the tank without spilling any sap. [14]I'm just tall enough. [15]Then I hang the pail back on that tree and walk to the next tree. [16]When the tank is full, Prancer pulls us to the sugar shack. [17]We drain the sap into the pans. [18]It will be boiled and made into syrup. [19]Then we go back and collect sap until all the buckets have been emptied. [20]Finally, I go home for a cup of hot chocolate.

DIRECTIONS: Circle the letter next to the correct answer or write the answer on the lines given. When asked, write the number of the sentence or the letter of the paragraph that is the best evidence.

1. The sled is powered by:
   A. motor
   B. pedals
   C. animal
   D. the sun

   Which 2 sentences from paragraph A are the best evidence? ____, ____

2. When does the story action take place?
   A. weekend
   B. holiday
   C. school day
   D. not known

3. What does the narrator mean by "what can Ma say?" in sentence 8?
   A. He wonders what she could say.
   B. She can't complain that he's wet.
   C. She wants him to come home.
   D. He thinks she wants him soaked.

4. What kind of liquid is in the bucket?

   _____

   Which sentence from paragraph C is the best evidence? ____

5. What kind of syrup will they have after the sap is boiled?
   A. apple
   B. corn
   C. pine
   D. maple

   Which sentence is the best evidence? ____

6. Read sentence 16. What must happen before the sled goes to the sugar shack?
   A. All buckets must be gathered.
   B. Sap must be gathered until the tank is filled.
   C. One more bucket must be poured.
   D. The sled must be pulled to the sugar shack.

5. **Teeger** by Margaret Hockett

A [1]He was the best friend she'd ever had. [2]But Mom wouldn't let Cari take him out of the house. [3]"He'll get dirty," she'd say. [4]So Teeger stayed in. [5]The orange body with the button eyes stayed in. [6]The soft "grrr" that only she could hear stayed in. [7]And all through the school day she'd think of his lonely smile.

B [8]One day, Teeger surprised her. [9]He was sitting up on the bed reading one of her books. [10]She could tell because he had on her mother's reading glasses. [11]The book was on the pillow.

C [12]On the next day, Teeger went as far as the kitchen. [13]He was having a bowl of corn flakes. [14]At least the bowl and spoon were beside him.

D [15]When Cari came home on the third day, she found Teeger in the living room. [16]He was sitting at the piano with his paws on the keyboard. [17]"I wondered where that beautiful music was coming from," Cari thought.

E [18]She smiled. [19]Maybe Teeger couldn't go outside, but at least he was finally enjoying himself. [20]"Thank you, Mom!" she exclaimed.

DIRECTIONS: Circle the letter next to the correct answer or write the answer on the lines given. When asked, write the number of the sentence or the letter of the paragraph that is the best evidence.

1. What was Teeger?
   A. a housecat
   B. a classmate
   C. a zoo animal
   D. a toy tiger

   Which sentence is the best evidence? _____

2. How did Cari think Teeger felt while she was gone?

   _____

   _____

   Which paragraph is the best evidence? _____

3. Who most likely put the glasses on Teeger?
   A. Mom
   B. Cari
   C. Teeger
   D. no one

   Which sentence from paragraph E is the best evidence? _____

4. How did it make Cari feel to think that Teeger was doing new things around the house?
   A. sad
   B. happy
   C. angry
   D. lonely

   Which paragraph is the best evidence? _____

5. Which sentence in paragraph D suggests that Cari uses her imagination?

   Sentence _____

6. At the end of the story, Cari thanked her mother. She probably did this because she thought her mother:
   A. fed Teeger his meals.
   B. helped Teeger enjoy himself.
   C. didn't let Teeger outside.
   D. kept Teeger from getting dirty.

6. Lead On, Sacagawea by David White

A [1]Lewis and Clark blazed a new trail by land to the Pacific Ocean. [2]They hoped to find a way for fur traders to reach tribes in the West. [3]They also wanted to see if the new land would be a good place to settle.

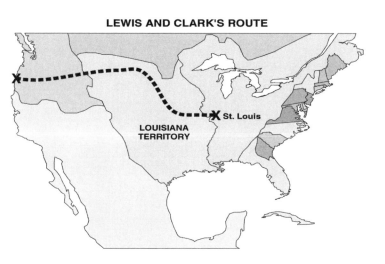

LEWIS AND CLARK'S ROUTE

LOUISIANA TERRITORY

St. Louis

B [4]Their trip took almost three years and covered 8,000 miles. [5]It began near St. Louis in May 1804. [6]They stopped in North Dakota for the winter. [7]During their stay, they hired a Native American guide. [8]Her name was Sacagawea.

C [9]Lewis and Clark were white and spoke only English. [10]Alone, they might not have been welcomed by the tribes. [11]They thought Sacagawea would be a big help to them. [12]She spoke two Native American languages. [13]She had family living in the West who could get them supplies. [14]She also knew the safest paths and rivers to take.

D [15]She had just given birth to a baby boy. [16]She carried the baby on her back the whole way. [17]They found that having a woman and baby with them let the tribes know that they were a friendly group.

E [18]The group started west in the spring. [19]They traveled on foot over the tall mountains, which were snowy even then. [20]They traveled by boat when they could to save time.

F [21]The explorers reached the west coast in the winter of 1805. [22]They headed home the next spring. [23]Lewis and Clark brought back new, important facts about the land in the West, its plants and animals, and its native peoples.

DIRECTIONS: Circle the letter next to the correct answer or write the answer on the lines given. When asked, write the number of the sentence or the letter of the paragraph that is the best evidence.

1. Sacagawea spoke two Native American languages. Why did Lewis and Clark think this would help?

   _____

   _____

   _____

   Which 2 sentences are the best evidence? ____, ____

2. Which of these might be another reason Lewis and Clark hired Sacagawea to lead them west?
   A. She could get them fresh food.
   B. She could carry extra supplies for them.
   C. She knew how to paddle a boat.
   D. She knew how to use native plants.

   Which sentence is the best evidence? ____

3. Why did the explorers NOT cross the mountains in winter?

   _____

   _____

   _____

   Which sentence is the best evidence? ____

4. Which of these probably best explains why the explorers traveled by boat in some places?
   A. They were more comfortable in boats than on horses.
   B. The boats had more room for supplies than the horses did.
   C. The rivers went directly to the west coast.
   D. It was usually faster than traveling on land.

   Which sentence is the best evidence? ____

5. What does sentence 3 suggest about travelers who would go west after Lewis and Clark?
   A. They would go in pairs.
   B. They would go there to stay.
   C. They would follow the same route.
   D. They would take Native American guides.

7. *The Barn* by Avi (Excerpt)

A   ¹"He seems the same to me," Harrison finally said.

B   ²"Wait," I told him. ³Then I drew the chair up as I had done before. ⁴Kneeling on it, I leaned close. ⁵"Father!" I shouted. ⁶"It's me, Ben!"

C   ⁷Father's fingers twitched some. ⁸And his feet stirred a bit.

D   ⁹"Ben," Nettie said, "this is foolishness."

E   ¹⁰"Wait!" I shouted, but at them, not at Father. ¹¹"Father!" I cried anew, and I stretched out my hand toward Nettie. ¹²"This is Nettie. ¹³If you know her, blink your eyes!"

F   ¹⁴His eyes shifted, his tongue flopped, and spit bubbled from his mouth. ¹⁵I wondered if I had been mistaken.

G   ¹⁶Harrison turned away. ¹⁷"I have work to do," he said.

H   ¹⁸"Father!" I screamed. ¹⁹"Show Nettie that you know it's her! ²⁰That you know your daughter! ²¹Close your eyes! ²²Close them to show you know!"

I   ²³And he did.

J   ²⁴There was silence in the house as big as any sky. ²⁵Nettie, her voice suddenly in tatters, whispered, "Ben, that doesn't *mean*. ²⁶It's only wishing."

K   ²⁷I turned back to Father. ²⁸"Show them again, Father!" I shouted. ²⁹"Close your eyes to say you know it's your Nettie standing there."

L   ³⁰Once again he closed his eyes.

M   ³¹"Oh, mercy…," Nettie murmured.

N   ³²"Now blink if you see Harrison, Father. ³³I want you to do it for him! ³⁴Go on!"

O   ³⁵Father blinked.

P   ³⁶Nettie gasped, covered her face with her hands. ³⁷Harrison stared, his mouth agape. ³⁸I clapped my hands with glee.

DIRECTIONS: Circle the letter next to the correct answer or write the answer on the lines given. When asked, write the number of the sentence or the letter of the paragraph that is the best evidence.

1. In sentence 9, what does Nettie think is foolish?

    _____

    _____

    Which paragraph is the best evidence? _____

2. How does Ben probably feel in paragraph F?
    - **A.** happy
    - **B.** strong
    - **C.** unsure
    - **D.** mad

    Which sentence is the best evidence? _____

3. Why do you think Ben asked Father to close his eyes in paragraph K and then move them again in paragraph N?
    - **A.** He wasn't sure if Father heard him the first time.
    - **B.** He wanted them to believe Father understood them.
    - **C.** He was proud that his father could do it.
    - **D.** He didn't see Father blink the first time.

4. Why do you think Nettie said, "Oh, mercy...," in sentence 31?
    - **A.** She still didn't believe that her father could understand them.
    - **B.** She was frightened by Ben's shouting.
    - **C.** She believed that Father could hear them.
    - **D.** She was tired of playing foolish games with Father.

5. Why does Ben clap his hands with glee in the last sentence of the story?

    _____

    _____

    _____

8. *Sable* by Karen Hesse (Excerpt)

A   [1]"I can see she'd work wonders keeping down the rabbit population. [2]She any good as a watchdog?" Doc Winston asked.

B   [3]"Sure is," Pap answered. [4]"She knows how to keep her eye on things, doesn't she, Tate?"

C   [5]I had a real uneasy feeling about what was happening here.

D   [6]"Look, if you're really thinking about giving her up," Doc Winston said, "I might take her."

E   [7]Something twisted inside me.

F   [8]"Would you?" Pap asked.

G   [9]"Pap!"

H   [10]"Listen, Tate," Pap said. [11]"We couldn't find a better home for her than here."

I   [12]"I've been thinking about getting another dog. [13]It's been years since we lost Damon," Doc Winston said.

J   [14]Pap nodded.

K   [15]"You wouldn't need to worry about her, Tate," Doc Winston told me. [16]"And you could come back to visit her anytime."

L   [17]Black specks floated in front of my eyes. [18]Come back to visit her! [19]She was my dog!

M   [20]"What do you think, Sable?" Doc Winston asked, stooping down. [21]"You want to stay? [22]You'd have a good home here. [23]Plenty room to run."

N   [24]I turned and glared at Pap.

O   [25]Sable sat panting softly in the green grass, surrounded by Doc Winston's land. [26]She held her sleek brown head high, gazing into the distance.

P   [27]"Good dog," Doc Winston said, running an admiring hand down her.

Q   [28]I couldn't watch anymore. [29]I ran to Pap's truck and slammed myself inside.

DIRECTIONS: Circle the letter next to the correct answer or write the answer on the lines given. When asked, write the number of the sentence or the letter of the paragraph that is the best evidence.

1. Sable is not only a good watchdog, she is also:

   A. a smart dog.
   B. a good runner.
   C. a good hunter.
   D. a small dog.

   Which sentence is the best evidence? ____

2. How is Tate feeling in sentences 5 and 7?

   A. uncaring
   B. worried
   C. sorry
   D. pleased

3. Which two sentences support the idea that Doc will give Sable a good home?

   Sentences ____, ____

4. Based on the story, which of the following is true about Doc?

   A. He used to have a dog.
   B. He used to have a cat.
   C. He doesn't like animals.
   D. He likes to hunt rabbits.

   Which 2 sentences are the best evidence? ____, ____

5. Where do you think Doc probably lives?

   A. in the country
   B. in an apartment
   C. at the beach
   D. on an island

   Which sentence is the best evidence? ____

DEFINING VOCABULARY USING CONTEXT

Using Context Clues in a Sentence

When reading a story, you may see a word you don't know. How can you figure out what this new word means? You could try using context clues. Context is the other words in a sentence that help give a word meaning.

1. The girls **adorned** their hair with flowers and ribbons.

In the sentence above, the words *flowers and ribbons* are clues. We can guess that the girls *put* flowers and ribbons in their hair. So the word *adorned* probably means to decorate. They probably did this to make themselves look pretty. So *adorned* also means to make something beautiful.

Sometimes a sentence will describe the meaning of a word for you. Look at the following example.

2. The **murmur** of the stream could barely be heard.

The words *could barely be heard* tell you that a murmur is a sound. In this sentence, it is the sound a stream is making. Since a stream is always moving, it is probably making a constant or steady sound. Since it can be barely heard, it is also a soft sound. So, *murmur* most likely means a soft, steady sound.

When you think you know what a word means, try to use another word or group of words with that meaning in place of the first word. In the sentence above, we think that *murmur* means a soft, steady sound. Replace the word *murmur* with these words. Does the sentence still make sense? If it does, you are probably on the right track. If it doesn't make sense, look at the context clues again.

Using context clues from the sentence, what do you think the word *disheveled* means in the following sentence?

3. His **disheveled** hair looked as if a bird had tried to make a nest in it.

Using Other Kinds of Context Clues

Other types of clues can help you define a word. Punctuation can be a clue. Look at the following sentence.

4.   There was **perspiration,** or sweat, dripping from his hot face.

The commas in the sentence are a clue that the words between them describe the word *perspiration*. In this case, the word *sweat* is given as another word for perspiration. The meaning of perspiration as sweat is also supported by the fact that the person is hot and dripping.

Other kinds of punctuation can also give clues. Parentheses ( ) can be used to set apart words that give meaning to another word. An exclamation mark gives you a clue about a character's mood or feelings.

Other kinds of context clues that you can use are the title of the story, what the characters say and do, and even pictures.

Look at the example below. What clues are you given that the word *railed* means shouted?

5.   "You won't get away with this!" the angry man **railed** at the children.

Using Context Clues in Other Sentences

Context clues can also be words in other sentences that help you figure out the meaning of a new word.

6.   [1]We were upset by the **cancellation** of the game. [2]It was the last game of the season. [3]We wouldn't get another chance to play. [4]Why did it have to rain!

The first sentence does not give you much information about the word *cancellation* except to tell you that they were upset about it. Sentence 3 gives you more information. It tells you that they will not get to play again. Sentence 4 gives you a reason for the cancellation, it rained. Using these clues, you can guess that the word *cancellation* may mean the game was called off or stopped. Put these words in place of *cancellation* to see if the sentence still makes sense: We were so upset by the *calling off* of the game.

VOCABULARY PRACTICE ACTIVITY

Activity 1

Read the following sentence. Then read the first question and circle the letter of the correct answer.

She **squinted** her eyes in the bright sunlight, trying to see the baby bird.

1. Which of the following words means almost the same as *squinted*?
   - **A.** partly closed
   - **B.** widened
   - **C.** completely closed
   - **D.** rolled

Look at the words *in the bright sunlight* in the sentence. If the sun is really bright, which choice makes more sense, A or B? Try putting each word or phrase in place of the word *squinted*.

Now look at the words *trying to see the baby bird.* If she was trying to look at something, which choice make more sense, A or C?

Look at choices A and D. Which is a better choice?

Activity 2

Read the following paragraph. Then answer question 2.

¹The storm **destroyed** the town. ²Buildings fell down. ³Water pipes burst and flooded the streets. ⁴People were hurt.

2. Which of the following words means almost the same as *destroyed?* Circle the letter next to the correct answer.
   - **A.** built
   - **B.** helped
   - **C.** wrecked
   - **D.** followed

Sentence 1 tells you that a storm did the *destroying*. But it doesn't tell you what the storm did. You have to look at the other sentences to figure out the meaning of the word *destroyed*.

Try putting *built* in place of destroyed in sentence 1. Now read sentence 2. Did the storm build the town if its buildings fell down?

Try putting *helped* in place of destroyed. Read sentences 2 and 3. Does the word *helped* make sense in the paragraph?

This leaves choices C and D. Which one makes sense in the paragraph?

Which two sentences gave you context clues that helped you with the meaning of the word *destroyed?* Write the numbers of the two sentences that give the best context clues. ____, ____

9. **Frontier Women** by Cheryl Block

A ¹In the 1800s, families started moving out west to **settle** the new land. ²They planned to make new homes there. ³They went in covered wagons. ⁴The trip was long and hard.

B ⁵Women had lots of work to do on the **journey** west. ⁶They gathered wood. ⁷They cooked and washed. ⁸They set up tents and fed the animals. ⁹Sometimes they even drove the wagons.

C ¹⁰Settling the new land was hard work, too. ¹¹First the land had to be **cleared.** ¹²Both women and men chopped down trees and removed rocks. ¹³Then there was room to build homes and plant crops.

D ¹⁴There were no stores where they could buy things. ¹⁵The settlers had to grow their own food. ¹⁶Women worked in the fields. ¹⁷Many women also knew how to hunt. ¹⁸Women made the clothing. ¹⁹They even made the cloth. ²⁰They also made their own soap and candles.

E ²¹Children as young as four or five years old did **chores**. ²²Young girls would fix meals and clean house. ²³They looked after the younger children. ²⁴Older girls helped to plant food crops and take care of animals. ²⁵There was very little time to play. ²⁶They made their work seem fun instead.

DIRECTIONS: Circle the letter next to the correct answer or write the answer on the lines given. When asked, write the number of the sentence or the letter of the paragraph that is the best evidence.

1. Which of the following words means almost the same as *settle* in sentences 1 and 10?

   A. enjoy
   B. stay on
   C. pay for
   D. discover

   Which other sentence from paragraph A gives the best context clue? ____

2. What does the word *journey* mean in sentence 5?

   _____

   _____

   Which other sentence from paragraph A gives the best context clue? ____

3. In sentence 11, what is meant by "the land had to be *cleared*"?

   _____

   _____

   Which other sentence gives the best context clue? ____

4a. In paragraph E, how do you know that the word *chores* means jobs?

   _____

   _____

4b. Write an example of a chore from paragraph E.

   _____

   _____

10. Lizard On the Loose by Cheryl Block

A [1]Mei brought her new pet lizard to school for show and tell. [2]The lizard was inside a shoebox. [3]Mei had punched air holes in the lid. [4]She also had a large rock and some grass inside the box.

B [5]Mei put the box on the floor when it was her turn to share. [6]She **cautiously** opened the lid to make sure the lizard didn't jump out. [7]It was sitting in a corner of the box. [8]The kids were crowding around and pushing to see better. [9]Someone accidentally **jostled** Ernie, and his foot hit the box. [10]It tipped over on its side. [11]Out ran the lizard.

C [12]The kids jumped back in surprise. [13]Mei bent down to pick up the lizard. [14]It ran away, and some of the kids **pursued** it. [15]They couldn't catch it. [16]Other kids, and even Mrs. Woods, climbed on their seats! [17]Kids continued to pursue the lizard as it ran around the room. [18]Mei was afraid someone would step on it.

D [19]Just then Mr. Purdy, the janitor, came in. [20]He had heard the **commotion** in the classroom from the hallway. [21]He took out his broom and dustpan. [22]Gently he scooped the lizard into the dustpan. [23]He held it in place under the broom. [24]Mei ran over to him with the shoebox. [25]She put the lizard back inside. [26]Mei was **elated** that her lizard was safe!

DIRECTIONS: Circle the letter next to the correct answer or write the answer on the lines given. When asked, write the number of the sentence or the letter of the paragraph that is the best evidence.

1. Which part of sentence 6 helps you figure out that *cautiously* means carefully?

   _____

   _____

2. Which word below can be used instead of *jostled* in sentence 9?

   A. held
   B. bumped
   C. liked
   D. missed

   Which other sentence gives the best context clue? _____

3. Paragraph C says some of the kids *pursued* the lizard. What did these kids do to the lizard?

   _____

   _____

4. What do you think a *commotion* is in sentence 20?

   A. classroom
   B. party
   C. bell
   D. noise

5. Which of the following is the best meaning for the word *elated* in sentence 26?

   A. worried
   B. sorry
   C. joyful
   D. quiet

11. George Washington Comes to Class by Margaret Hockett

A [1]Mr. Yates was **droning on** about the Father of Our Country. [2]He was telling that boring old story about chopping down the cherry tree. [3]My eyelids were getting heavy and starting to fall. [4]They were **descending** along with the cherry tree.

B [5]Then I heard a new voice.

C [6]When I looked up again, Mr. Yates had changed. [7]He was taller, and his hair was white. [8]He had blue-gray eyes. [9]They seemed to **pierce** us like arrows.

D [10]"Don't believe others," he began. [11]"If you want to know the truth, ask me."

E [12]I asked, "You didn't have video games or snowboards as a kid, did you? [13]What did you do for excitement?"

F [14]"I loved wrestling and dancing." [15]His eyes sparkled with mischief. [16]"I even went to the races at times."

G [17]He thought for a moment. [18]"But the most fun was camping out. [19]When I went on a trip to measure borders, I did more than **survey** the land. [20]I had to survive in the woods. [21]The scary part came when I met some Indians. [22]They were wearing war paint! [23]I was glad to make it home all right...all right..."

H [24]"...all right?" [25]Mr. Yates was asking if I was okay. [26]My head had thumped to the desk. [27]"You fell just like the tree in my story!" he exclaimed.

I [28]"I'm fine," I replied, slowly raising my head. [29]"But you can forget the cherry tree. [30]Now I can tell you about the *real* George Washington!"

DIRECTIONS: Circle the letter next to the correct answer or write the answer on the lines given. When asked, write the number of the sentence or the letter of the paragraph that is the best evidence.

1. Sentence 1 uses the words *droning on*. Choose the words that come closest to the meaning of *droning on*.

   A. speaking in a dull voice
   B. speaking with love
   C. speaking excitedly
   D. speaking as if singing

   Which sentence gives the best context clue? _____

2a. As used in sentence 4, what does the word *descending* mean?

   _____

2b. Which part of sentence 3 gives you a clue to the meaning of *descending*?

   _____

   _____

3. In sentence 9, the word *pierce* means *go through*. What part of sentence 9 gives you a clue to the meaning of *pierce*?

   _____

   _____

4. Which part of sentence 19 gives you a clue to the meaning of *survey*?

   _____

   _____

12. **Desert Survivor** by Cheryl Block

A   [1]The cactus is an unusual plant. [2]It can last a long time without water. [3]How does it do this?

B   [4]Some cactus plants have one very long main root. [5]It can be as long as 15 feet. [6]This root goes deep under the ground to reach water. [7]Other cactus plants have lots of roots that are **shallow**. [8]They spread out from the plant and stay near the surface. [9]These shallow roots can take in water from even a light rain because they are not deep.

C   [10]The stem of a cactus is made to store water. [11]The inside of the stem acts like a sponge. [12]When it rains, the cactus stem **absorbs** the rain through its outer skin and holds it inside. [13]Some cactus stems have ridges along their sides that **expand** to let the stem hold even more water. [14]As it rains, the expanding sides of these cactuses grow bigger. [15]The outer skin of a cactus stem is often thick and waxy to help keep in water.

DIRECTIONS: Circle the letter next to the correct answer or write the answer on the lines given. When asked, write the number of the sentence or the letter of the paragraph that is the best evidence.

1. The word *shallow* most likely means:

   A. near the surface.
   B. deep underground.
   C. full of water.
   D. spread out.

2. Which part of sentence 9 helps you understand what *shallow* means?

   A. can take in water
   B. from even a light rain
   C. are not deep
   D. these shallow roots

3. Write the part of sentence 8 that helps you understand what *shallow* means.

   _____

   _____

4. Which of the following means almost the same as *absorbs* in sentence 12?

   A. throws away
   B. squeezes
   C. takes in
   D. replaces

5. Write the part of sentence 14 that helps explain the meaning of the word *expand* in sentence 13.

   _____

   _____

13. **New World for the Old** by Margaret Hockett

A [1]Old people were disappearing.

B [2]Meg Walsh was first. [3]But she was always coming and going anyway, so no one noticed right away. [4]Then it was Mitzy Piper, 'ole Ryan, and Sawed-Off Henson. [5]Later, others would join the list of missing **elderly** people.

C [6]Where had they gone? [7]Little Bipsy Henson found the first clue. [8]She **glimpsed** a face in a hollow stump in the woods. [9]When she looked again, the face was gone. [10]Helen Hiller heard humming noises at the same place.

D [11]We went to check it out. [12]**Investigating** the inside of the dark stump, I felt a ledge. [13]I pushed. [14]A trapdoor opened! [15]I lowered my head through it and looked. [16]No one could have ever guessed what I saw.

E [17]It was an underground wonderland! [18]Many unusual inventions met my eyes. [19]Since no two things were alike, it was quite an **assortment**. [20]Whirligigs whirled. [21]Robots robotted.

F [22]The old people let us in, but only because we were kids.

G [23]"Why did you leave?" we asked.

H [24]Meg replied, "The other adults wanted us to rest. [25]They thought we should be taken care of."

I [26]"But isn't that good?" Beany asked.

J [27]"Not really," Meg answered. [28]"You see, they thought we were no longer useful."

K [29]Buddy Chung added, "Nobody took us seriously. [30]We know more than they think. [31]And the ideas! [32]Boy we've got a bunch of 'em."

L [33]So we never told the adults what happened to the old folks. [34]They just **assumed** that when they got older, they too would disappear. [35]They didn't know *where* they would go, they just knew they would go.

M [36]And you know what? [37]They did.

N [38]Then there would be a new bed in the forest wonderland. [39]And a new **resident** to fill it.

DIRECTIONS: Circle the letter next to the correct answer or write the answer on the lines given. When asked, write the number of the sentence or the letter of the paragraph that is the best evidence.

1. What is the meaning of the word *elderly*, as used in sentence 5?

    A. aged
    B. human
    C. sad
    D. unwanted

    Which other sentence gives the best context clue? _____

2. The word *glimpsed* in sentence 8 means to have a quick look. Write the part of sentence 9 that supports this meaning.

    _____

3a. In sentence 12, the word *investigating* means:

    A. seeing.
    B. running away from.
    C. pushing.
    D. checking out.

3b. Which two sentences together give the best evidence?

    A. 14, 15
    B. 15, 16
    C. 11, 12
    D. 13, 14

4. Sentence 19 uses the word *assortment*. If you had an *assortment* of toys, they would probably all:

    A. be the same.
    B. have movable parts.
    C. look new and unusual.
    D. be different.

    Write the part of sentence 19 that gives you a clue to the answer.

    _____

    _____

5. If you *assumed* something, as in paragraph L, you would probably:

    A. think it was true.
    B. think it was wrong.
    C. grow old.
    D. disappear.

6. A *resident* (sentence 39) is probably:

    A. someone who lives in a place.
    B. someone who gets lost easily.
    C. one of many robots.
    D. one of many whirligigs.

14. Help Solve the Garbage Problem by Carrie Beckwith

A   [1]When you throw something away, where does it go? [2]It doesn't just go away. [3]Most of our garbage is buried in the ground. [4]Sometimes it is dumped in the ocean. [5]Right now, we have too much garbage. [6]In order to fix this problem, we need to **reduce** the amount of garbage we make. [7]You can begin by doing three things.

B   [8]First, <u>try not to buy things that use lots of paper and plastic</u>. [9]For example, buy a big bottle of apple juice rather than a small six-pack. [10]The six-pack uses six small bottles plus cardboard. [11]The big bottle is only one bottle. [12]Then you can reuse the bottle to store cold water in the refrigerator. [13]Or, turn it into a vase for flowers.

C   [14]Second, **recycle** <u>the garbage that you do make</u>. [15]When you recycle something, you are using it again. [16]Materials like paper, plastic, and glass can be recycled. [17]City recycling centers are great places to leave your old paper, plastic, or glass. [18]When you recycle, you are making sure that nothing is thrown away to become garbage.

D   [19]Last, you can <u>create a compost pile in your backyard</u>. [20]A compost pile is a place to put **organic** materials. [21]Organic materials are things that were once alive and growing. [22]Bread, for example, comes from wheat that once grew in fields. [23]Grass clippings once grew from the earth. [24]So, vegetable scraps, grass, and dead leaves can be thrown into your pile. [25]Turn over the materials with a rake about once a week. [26]Over time, the materials will **decay.** [27]As the materials decay, they break down and turn into new soil.

E   [28]You can help the garbage problem. [29]Cut down the amount of trash you make. [30]Recycle things that can be used again. [31]Make a compost pile. [32]*You* can make a difference!

DIRECTIONS: Circle the letter next to the correct answer or write the answer on the lines given. When asked, write the number of the sentence or the letter of the paragraph that is the best evidence.

1. Write the three words from sentence 15 that best show the meaning of the word *recycle*.

   _____

   _____

2. The word *reduce* in sentence 6 means:

   A. add to.
   B. bury.
   C. lessen.
   D. burn.

   Which other sentence from paragraph A gives you a clue to the answer? _____

3a. Read the definition of *organic* in sentence 21. Which of the following is NOT made of organic materials?

   A. wooden comb
   B. plastic cup
   C. watermelon
   D. pea soup

3b. Circle the items below that *are* organic.

   coffee grounds

   color photo

   pine needles

   banana peel

   nail polish

4. Using sentence 27, you can tell that the word *decay* means:

   A. start growing.
   B. break down.
   C. stay the same.
   D. turn into flowers.

STORY PARTS

Identifying Story Parts

A story is composed of parts that hold it together. Each of the following parts is important to the development of the story.

Plot

The plot is the series of events that take place in the story. Every plot has a beginning, a middle, and an end. For instance, in the story of "The Three Little Pigs," the plot of the story is how the three pigs try to escape from the wolf. Each one builds a different house. Only one house is left standing at the end.

Most plots begin with a problem, or conflict. In "The Three Little Pigs," the conflict is between the wolf and the pigs.

Conflict

A conflict is the main problem in the story. There may be a conflict between one character and another. Sometimes the conflict is between a character and something else, such as nature. A character can even have an inner conflict where he or she isn't sure what to do.

Read the following story. What is the conflict in the story?

1. [1]It was turning darker and colder. [2]He stumbled through the brush. [3]Thorny branches scratched him and tore at his clothes. [4]He jumped when he heard a rustling in the bushes. [5]A coyote howled in the distance, and the boy shivered. [6]He was thirsty, but he no longer knew where the river was. [7]Soon he wouldn't be able to see anything. [8]Would anyone come to find him?

The conflict is between the boy and nature. He is lost in the woods and must try to survive alone in the wilderness. Sentence 1 tells us he must face darkness and cold. Sentence 5 mentions a wild animal. Sentence 6 tells us he is thirsty and has no water.

Identifying Setting

The setting is the time and place in which a story takes place. Sometimes you are told the exact time and place. Other times, there may be clues that suggest when and where the story happens. What is the setting in the following story?

2. ¹As they stood inside, they could look down on the whole neighborhood. ²They pulled up the rope ladder so no one would know they were up there. ³It was Saturday morning. ⁴Mrs. Perkins was hanging her wash. ⁵Mr. Fuji was washing his car. ⁶There went Sammy on his roller blades. ⁷Jasmine whistled at him and then ducked beneath the open window. ⁸Sammy looked around. ⁹But no one could see them hidden up there in the tree's leafy branches.

Sentence 3 tells you that the time is Saturday morning. From clues given in the story, you can guess that the kids are probably in a tree house. Sentence 1 suggests they are up high. Sentence 2 tells you they used a rope ladder to get where they are. Sentence 7 suggests they are in a house. Sentence 9 tells you they are up in the tree branches.

There are other elements of setting that are important, too. Weather is part of the story setting. A storm, for instance, may affect the action in the story. Time can mean different things:

- The time of day

- The length of time that passes. A story may follow one brief event or a character's whole life.

- The historical time period. This is especially important in stories that take place in the past or the future.

During what time period does the following story take place?

3. ¹Ramses put down his tools and took a drink of water. ²The desert sun was hot. ³He had been helping his father all morning. ⁴It was hard work cutting the stone blocks. ⁵A single block stood taller than Ramses. ⁶He was amazed that the workers could move the huge blocks at all. ⁷He could see the giant pyramid taking shape as he looked around. ⁸The great Pharaoh would be pleased.

Analyzing Characters

Characters' words and actions keep a story moving. These words and actions can also tell you about a character's traits, or what kind of person he or she is. Traits describe a person's qualities. A character may be kind or mean, silly or serious, brave or timid.

Read the following passage.

4. ¹"Has anyone seen my new pen?" asked Mrs. Chan. ²"I know it was right here a minute ago." ³As I looked at her desk I had no idea where "right here" might be. ⁴There wasn't an empty space anywhere. ⁵Some piles were a foot deep. ⁶Mrs. Chan never threw out anything. ⁷Who knew what lurked in those desk drawers? ⁸The last time I helped her look for something, I found last month's birthday cake still sitting on a plate.

What character trait would you use to describe Mrs. Chan?
  A. funny
  B. messy
  C. tidy
  D. strict

How does the evidence in the paragraph support your choice?

A story's conflict may center on one or two characters. A character may become a hero who saves everyone. A bad character may become good during the story. You learn what a character is like as you watch what he does and says.

In the following story, what kind of person is Arthur? What clues do you find from his actions?

5. ¹Arthur wants to be first in line. ²When the bell rings, he runs as fast as he can to line up. ³He pushes people out of his way. ⁴He even knocks Taima to the ground and keeps on going. ⁵When Kiri arrives there before him, he tries to push her out of line.

STORY PARTS PRACTICE ACTIVITY

Read the following story. Then answer the questions.

A ¹Sarah and her family were visiting relatives in New England. ²They were spending the night in Oakley Manor. ³Sarah's aunt and uncle had just bought the old house. ⁴They planned to fix it up and turn it into an inn.

B ⁵In the middle of the night, Sarah was awakened by a low wailing sound. ⁶She climbed out of bed and grabbed her flashlight from the nightstand. ⁷She peeked out the door. ⁸No one else was awake.

C ⁹She walked down the dark hall. ¹⁰The wailing grew louder. ¹¹Who could it be? ¹²Was someone in pain? ¹³The sound was coming from behind a locked door at the end of the hall. ¹⁴Should she wake up her parents? ¹⁵As she turned away, the door creaked open. ¹⁶Sarah looked inside. ¹⁷There was a narrow stairway leading up to the attic. ¹⁸The wailing was coming from up there. ¹⁹Should she go up alone?

1. Where does the story take place?
   A. in an old house in New England
   B. in an inn in Oakley, England
   C. in Sarah's family home
   D. in a hotel in New England

   Which paragraph is the best evidence? _____

2. When does the story take place?

   _____

   Which sentence is the best evidence? _____

3. How would you describe Sarah?

    A. shy

    B. sad

    C. friendly

    D. curious

Look at paragraph C. What is Sarah doing? Does choice A or B make more sense? How about C or D?

4a. What is Sarah's conflict in the story?

_____

The conflict in the story is between Sarah and herself. What decision is Sarah trying to make in paragraph C?

_____

4b. Which of the following sentences is the best evidence? You may choose more than one.

    A. Was someone in pain?

    B. Should she wake up her parents?

    C. The wailing was coming from up there.

    D. Should she go up alone?

15. A View From Above by David White

A ¹I'm up in a balloon. ²The air is taking me higher. ³Clouds float by. ⁴I pull on a cord to make the balloon stop rising. ⁵I fly straight.

B ⁶I can see for miles. ⁷I look to the left and see two mountain peaks, both covered with snow. ⁸Below the peaks are grass-covered hills. ⁹Leaves are changing colors. ¹⁰I look to the right and see the ocean. ¹¹Far in the distance I can see an island. ¹²I look below me and see a curving river. ¹³Farms dot the landscape. ¹⁴There is so much to see as the hours fly by.

C ¹⁵It is so quiet up here. ¹⁶I can hear the wind whispering. ¹⁷Every so often I hear an insect whiz by or a goose honking. ¹⁸It's the time of year when geese head for warmer places. ¹⁹It's not really cold yet, but geese know best.

D ²⁰I've been in the air for about four hours now, and I want it to be longer. ²¹Sunset is approaching. ²²The sky is turning a fantastic shade of red. ²³I take out my camera and snap a few shots. ²⁴I want to remember how the sky looks from way up here.

E ²⁵It's time to touch down. ²⁶I don't want to, but I have to. ²⁷I pull on the cord. ²⁸The balloon drops slowly to the ground. ²⁹Touchdown is a little bumpy, but I'm OK. ³⁰I have a great story to tell.

DIRECTIONS: Circle the letter next to the correct answer or write the answer on the lines given. When asked, write the number of the sentence or the letter of the paragraph that is the best evidence.

1. From where is the narrator telling the story?

   _____

   Which sentence is the best evidence? ____

2. Summarize the plot.

   _____

   _____

   _____

3. What is the conflict described in paragraph E?

   _____

   _____

   Which sentence is the best evidence? ____

4. Number the following events in the order in which they happened in the story.

   ____ narrator sees island

   ____ balloon touches down

   ____ sun begins to set

   ____ balloon flies straight

   ____ narrator takes pictures

5. What do we learn about the narrator from the story?
   A. He likes to watch birds.
   B. He enjoys nature.
   C. He is a painter.
   D. He is afraid of heights.

6. What time of year is it in the story?
   A. spring
   B. summer
   C. fall
   D. winter

   Give one sentence each from paragraphs B and C that is the best evidence. ____, ____

16. A Foolish Wish by Cheryl Block

A   [1]A young lad was going to market to sell some eggs. [2]On the way, he spotted a shiny object in the road. [3]He bent down to pick it up. [4]It was a gold coin!

B   [5]The boy was thrilled. [6]He couldn't believe his good luck. [7]As he walked along, he thought of all the things he could buy in town. [8]He had never had so much money.

C   [9]When he came to the edge of town, he stopped at the well for a drink of water. [10]Some people thought it was a wishing well. [11]They believed that if you threw in a coin, your wish would come true. [12]The boy had never had a coin to throw in the well.

D   [13]The boy thought, "Why should I settle for just one gold coin when I could have many? [14]If I throw my gold coin into the well, I could be rich." [15]So he took his coin and threw it in the well. [16]Then he wished as hard as he could for more gold coins and waited. [17]Nothing happened. [18]He waited all day.

E   [19]Finally, it started to get dark. [20]The boy realized how foolish he had been. [21]His coin was gone, and so was his wish. [22]The market was now closed, so he couldn't sell his eggs. [23]Slowly, the boy walked home.

[24]Moral: A fool and his money are soon parted.

DIRECTIONS: Circle the letter next to the correct answer or write the answer on the lines given. When asked, write the number of the sentence or the letter of the paragraph that is the best evidence.

1. Where does the story take place?

_____

_____

_____

Which 2 sentences are the best evidence? ____, ____

2. Where is the well located?
   A. just outside town
   B. on a hill
   C. near his house
   D. in the middle of town

   Which sentence is the best evidence? ____

3. Which of the following is a main event in the story?
   A. He was thrilled.
   B. He found a coin.
   C. He was going to market.
   D. He walked back home.

4. Why was the boy foolish?

_____

_____

_____

Which 2 paragraphs are the best evidence? ____, ____

5. How did the boy probably feel at the end?
   A. cheerful
   B. disappointed
   C. uncaring
   D. frightened

   Which 2 sentences are the best evidence? ____, ____

6. Summarize the results of the boy's actions.

_____

_____

_____

Which paragraph is the best evidence? ____

17. First Wave by Carrie Beckwith

A ¹Jonah squeezed into his wetsuit. ²Dad waxed his surfboard. ³The early morning air was still. ⁴"The waves are small. ⁵You'll be fine," Jonah's dad said. ⁶"Yeah, they're small," Jonah repeated. ⁷But his heart didn't seem to believe him. ⁸It was pounding like a jackhammer.

B ⁹Dad picked up his board and jogged into the ocean. ¹⁰Jonah followed close behind. ¹¹They paddled past the breaking waves. ¹²Jonah kept looking back to the beach. ¹³It was no bigger than an anthill now.

C ¹⁴"Don't turn your head away from the ocean," Dad warned. ¹⁵"Stay alert." ¹⁶Dad sat up on his board and looked for a wave. ¹⁷"I see one coming. ¹⁸It'll be nice and easy." ¹⁹Jonah couldn't see a thing. ²⁰He wondered if the wave would catch him off guard. ²¹His stomach felt uneasy, like the moving water below.

D ²²"All right, Jonah. ²³Turn your board around. ²⁴I'll tell you when to go." ²⁵Jonah's heart was really pounding now. ²⁶He could hear the wave coming. ²⁷He twisted his head around to see it.

E ²⁸"Go! ²⁹Go now, Jonah! ³⁰Paddle fast!" ³¹Jonah dug his arms into the water. ³²The speed of the wave carried him fast. ³³He grabbed the sides of the board with his hands. ³⁴He lifted his body. ³⁵His feet came up and landed on the board! ³⁶"Yes!" Jonah screamed. ³⁷He bent his knees and let his arms hang low. ³⁸Finally, he was riding a wave.

DIRECTIONS: Circle the letter next to the correct answer or write the answer on the lines given. When asked, write the number of the sentence or the letter of the paragraph that is the best evidence.

1. Number the events of the story in correct time order.

   ____ Jonah puts on his wetsuit.

   ____ Jonah turns his board around.

   ____ Dad spots a wave.

   ____ Jonah gets his feet on the board.

2. In paragraph A, you can tell that Jonah is:

   A. nervous.
   B. silly.
   C. angry.
   D. bored.

   Which 2 sentences are the best evidence? ____, ____

3. What made Jonah scream "Yes!" in sentence 36?

   _____

   _____

   Which 2 sentences are the best evidence? ____, ____

4. Use paragraphs A and B to describe both the time and place of the story.

   _____

   _____

   _____

   _____

   Which 2 sentences from paragraphs A and B are the best evidence? ____, ____

5. What is Dad trying to do with Jonah?

   _____

   _____

   _____

18. Surprise Vacation by Carrie Beckwith

A   ¹Dad loved to have fun with us. ²One April morning my brother and I walked into the kitchen. ³Mom was making pancakes. ⁴Dad announced, "We're going to Hawaii. ⁵Pack your bags!" ⁶Our eyeballs almost popped out.

B   ⁷"We're going to Hawaii! ⁸We're going to Hawaii!" we sang. ⁹Mom gave Dad a funny look. ¹⁰Our big brother kept eating his cereal. ¹¹He didn't even lift his head. ¹²We ran into our rooms and packed. ¹³We stuffed our bags with all our games and clothes.

C   ¹⁴"Maybe we'll never come back!" I exclaimed.

D   ¹⁵"Maybe we'll never go back to school again," my brother added. ¹⁶We dragged our bags into the kitchen. ¹⁷Sean tripped over his bag twice.

E   ¹⁸"We're ready to go, Dad!" I said with a smile.

F   ¹⁹Dad was smiling too. ²⁰He handed us the calendar and pointed to the date. ²¹Our big brother lifted his head. ²²He started laughing. ²³Mom frowned. ²⁴Then she said, "Sweetheart, it's April Fool's Day."

G   ²⁵Dad had done it again.

DIRECTIONS: Circle the letter next to the correct answer or write the answer on the lines given. When asked, write the number of the sentence or the letter of the paragraph that is the best evidence.

1. Number the following events in the story in the correct time order.

    ____ Dad tells the family that they're going to Hawaii.

    ____ Sean trips over his bag on his way back to the kitchen.

    ____ Dad points to the date on the calendar.

    ____ The kids pack their bags.

2. Describe where most of the story takes place.

    _____

    _____

    Which 2 sentences are the best evidence? ____, ____

3. During what part of the day does the story take place?

    _____

    Which sentence is the best evidence? ____

4. You can guess from Dad's actions that he:

    A. is hard working.
    B. likes to joke.
    C. is very serious.
    D. likes to travel.

    Which 2 paragraphs are the best evidence? ____, ____

5. In paragraph B, how can you tell that the kids were happy about going to Hawaii? Give two examples.

    1. _____

    _____

    2. _____

    _____

    Which 2 sentences are the best evidence? ____, ____

6. What did their big brother do after Dad pointed to the date?

    _____

    _____

    Which 2 sentences are the best evidence? ____, ____

19. A Puff of Smoke by Cheryl Block

A ¹I almost threw the egg away. ²But something made me take it home. ³I wrapped a towel around it and put it in a box on my dresser. ⁴Then I forgot all about it.

B ⁵The next morning, I heard a tiny squeaking sound coming from the box. ⁶The egg had hatched! ⁷Inside was a tiny green dragon. ⁸Mom and Dad couldn't believe it when I showed them the dragon. ⁹They said I could keep it. ¹⁰I named him Dino.

C ¹¹At first, I kept Dino in the box. ¹²But he quickly outgrew it. ¹³He ate as much as a small horse. ¹⁴He was very fond of scrambled eggs.

D ¹⁵He kept growing and growing. ¹⁶He was almost five feet tall. ¹⁷He also had a long tail and wings. ¹⁸He started knocking things over with his tail. ¹⁹Mom was worried that he'd break something. ²⁰Dad decided to keep him in the back yard.

E ²¹The neighbors were surprised. ²²They didn't seem to mind until Dino started breathing fire. ²³At first, he only puffed smoke. ²⁴When he accidentally set fire to Mr. Mickles' tree, Mr. Mickles called the police. ²⁵The police said there wasn't any law against keeping a dragon in your back yard. ²⁶Dad said we'd watch him.

F ²⁷The neighborhood kids loved Dino. ²⁸He gave them rides on his back and roasted marshmallows for them. ²⁹Dino was also learning to fly.

G ³⁰Dino seemed sad, though. ³¹I knew he missed his family. ³²There were no other dragons around. ³³It was time for him to go and find them. ³⁴We all cried when Dino left. ³⁵But I knew he'd come back to visit. ³⁶And next time, he wouldn't be alone.

DIRECTIONS: Circle the letter next to the correct answer or write the answer on the lines given. When asked, write the number of the sentence or the letter of the paragraph that is the best evidence.

1. How did the parents first react to Dino?
   A. They were very angry.
   B. They were frightened.
   C. They were surprised.
   D. They weren't interested.

   Which sentence is the best evidence? ____

2. In what room did the boy put the egg?

   _____

   Which sentence is the best evidence? ____

3. What is the most important event in paragraph B?
   A. A squeaking sound wakes up the boy.
   B. The boy names the dragon Dino.
   C. A dragon hatches from the egg.
   D. The boy shows the dragon to his parents.

4. When did Dad move Dino to the back yard?
   A. when he outgrew the box
   B. after he hatched
   C. when he started knocking things over
   D. after he set Mr. Mickles' tree on fire

   Which sentence is the best evidence? ____

5. According to paragraph F, how would you describe Dino?
   A. gentle
   B. fierce
   C. shy
   D. silly

   Which 2 sentences are the best evidence? ____, ____

20. Invisible Spy by Margaret Hockett

A   [1]Maisy Pikes was a genius. [2]And she used her new invention to send the bad guys to jail.

B   [3]Some tough guys were making her dad pay them every week. [4]They would smash up his store if he didn't pay.

C   [5]Maisy was angry. [6]If only she could follow the men without being seen! [7]She could find their hideout and record their plans. [8]Then she could take the information to the police.

D   [9]She figured out how to do it. [10]By putting things together in a special way, she invented a machine to make her seem invisible.

E   [11]She wore a small movie camera on her back. [12]As she moved, the scene behind her was projected on her front side. [13]She was camouflaged!* [14]She seemed to be part of the background.

F   [15]Maisy followed the men into the park. [16]Stepping on a twig, she froze. [17]"Who's there?" the short one asked as he turned and looked right at her. [18]But he saw no one, and they went on. [19]She was shaking, but she followed them to their secret meeting place under a tree.

G   [20]She took a recording of their voices, and she took it to the cops.

H   [21]Now the criminals are in jail where they belong. [22]Her dad is happy. [23]The government is going to pay Maisy for her invention. [24]They want to develop the idea for military use.

I   [25]Maisy even got her picture in the newspaper. [26]But she insisted on wearing her new invention—and no one can find her in the photograph!

*camouflage: to hide something by making it look like part of the background

DIRECTIONS: Circle the letter next to the correct answer or write the answer on the lines given. When asked, write the number of the sentence or the letter of the paragraph that is the best evidence.

1. Which of the following is a key event in the story?
   A. Maisy is in the newspaper.
   B. Maisy steps on a twig.
   C. Maisy is paid by the government.
   D. Maisy puts her invention to use.

   Which 2 paragraphs are the best evidence? ____, ____

2a. Maisy could be described as a _____ kind of girl.
   A. wimpy
   B. crazy
   C. take-charge
   D. do-nothing

2b. Of the following sentences, which best supports your answer?
   A. 5
   B. 14
   C. 20
   D. 24

3. Describe the setting of the main action in the story.

   _____

   _____

   Which paragraph is the best evidence? ____

4. Number the following events in the order they happened in the story.

   ____ Mr. Pikes is threatened.

   ____ Bad guys go to jail.

   ____ Maisy steps on a twig.

   ____ Maisy goes to the cops.

5. The main conflict in the story is between Maisy and whom or what?

   _____

   _____

21. *Dexter* by Clyde Robert Bulla (Excerpt)

A   ¹If he could drive him deeper into the timber where Mr. Ogle couldn't find him…

B   ²He came to the creek. ³A man was there on the bank—Wayne's father in a red hunting jacket. ⁴He had a rifle in his hands.

C   ⁵On the other side of the creek was Dexter, his head up, his eyes watching.

D   ⁶"Don't!" cried Dave.

E   ⁷Mr. Ogle almost dropped the rifle. ⁸"What are you doing here?"

F   ⁹"Don't do it," said Dave. ¹⁰"You can't do it!"

G   ¹¹"Don't tell me what I can't do." ¹²Mr. Ogle lifted the rifle.

H   ¹³Dexter was still watching. ¹⁴He seemed to be waiting.

I   ¹⁵Mr. Ogle took aim. ¹⁶He stopped and rubbed his eyes. ¹⁷He said to Dave, "Go somewhere else. ¹⁸Go on—get out!"

J   ¹⁹He aimed again. ²⁰He took a step forward, almost as if he wanted to frighten the pony away. ²¹But Dexter stood quietly.

K   ²²Mr. Ogle was shaking. ²³He said, "Why does he have to keep looking at me? ²⁴I can't do it when he looks at me—when you both look at me!"

L   ²⁵He put the rifle over his shoulder and went stamping away. ²⁶Dave heard his steps in the dry leaves. ²⁷Then the timber was still.

M   ²⁸Dave felt weak. ²⁹There was a blur in front of his eyes. ³⁰When he could see again, he looked across the creek. ³¹Dexter was gone.

DIRECTIONS: Circle the letter next to the correct answer or write the answer on the lines given. When asked, write the number of the sentence or the letter of the paragraph that is the best evidence.

1. Where does the story take place?
   A. out in the open field
   B. in the deepest timber
   C. on the banks of a creek
   D. by the seashore

2a. The main conflict is between:
   A. Dave and himself
   B. Dexter and Dave
   C. Dexter and Mr. Ogle
   D. Dave and Mr. Ogle

2b. Explain the conflict.

   _____

   _____

   _____

   Which 2 paragraphs are the best evidence? ____, ____

3. Paragraph K shows that Mr. Ogle also has a conflict with himself. Describe the conflict.

   _____

   _____

4. What can you tell about Mr. Ogle from the passage?
   A. He lets nothing get in his way.
   B. He doesn't believe in killing.
   C. He is affected by others.
   D. He is a patient hunter.

   Which sentence is the best evidence? ____

5. What goal seems most important to Dave?
   A. saving the pony
   B. telling Mr. Ogle what to do
   C. driving the horses
   D. keeping people from hunting

6. Number the events in the order they happened.

   ____ Mr. Ogle tells Dave to go away.

   ____ Dave yells to stop Mr. Ogle.

   ____ Dave's eyes are blurred.

   ____ Mr. Ogle puts the rifle over his shoulder.

IDENTIFYING MAIN IDEA AND SUPPORTING DETAILS

Finding the Main Idea

A nonfiction article has a topic and a main idea. The topic tells you what the article is about, such as cooking or pioneer life. The main idea tells you what the author wants to say about the topic. An article usually has one main idea. Read the following article.

I   [1]Spiders are not insects. [2]They belong to the same class of animals as insects. [3]However, there are many differences between spiders and insects.

[4]The bodies of spiders and insects are different. [5]A spider's body has two main parts. [6]The front part is the head and chest together. [7]The second part is the stomach, or abdomen. [8]The insect's body has three parts. [9]In the insect, the head and chest are two separate parts. [10]The abdomen is the third part.

[11]There are other differences between a spider's body and an insect's body. [12]An insect has six legs. [13]A spider has eight legs. [14]Most insects also have wings and spiders don't. [15]An insect has antennae on its head. [16]A spider has no antennae.

The **topic** of the article is spiders. The main idea of an article is usually given in a **topic sentence** found in the first paragraph. The **main idea** of this article is in the first sentence: Spiders are not insects.

The paragraphs in an article support the main idea of the article. For instance, the second paragraph in the article above gives one reason why spiders are not insects. Each paragraph also has its own topic sentence with a main idea. The topic sentence is usually the first sentence of the paragraph. Sentence 4 is the topic sentence of the second paragraph. It tells us that spiders and insects have different bodies. The other sentences in the paragraph are **supporting details**. They tell us how the bodies are different. What is the topic sentence in the third paragraph?

Sometimes the topic sentence of a paragraph is not the first sentence. Read the following paragraph. Which sentence is the topic sentence?

2   ¹Phan put the last can in the box. ²They had almost 600 cans. ³Phan's class had won the pizza party for collecting the most cans in the school.

MAIN IDEA PRACTICE ACTIVITY

Read the following story. Then answer the questions.

[1]Imagine what it would be like if you didn't have any bones. [2]Your body would be soft and limp. [3]Your skeleton is the framework that supports and protects your body.

[4]Your skeleton has three important jobs. [5]It supports your body and gives it shape. [6]It protects organs inside your body, such as the heart and liver. [7]It holds the muscles that help your body move.

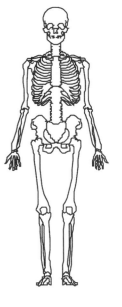

1. What is the main idea of the story?
    A. The skeleton is the framework for the body.
    B. The skeleton supports the body.
    C. The skeleton has three important jobs.
    D. The skeleton protects the heart and liver.

Think about each of the choices. Which one gives the most important idea in the story? Do the other sentences support this idea?

2. What is the main idea of the second paragraph?

    _____

3. Which sentences in the second paragraph are supporting details?

    _____

4. How does the second paragraph support the main idea of the story?

    _____

    _____

22. Your Sense of Taste by Carrie Beckwith

A [1]What makes ice cream taste so good? [2]Your nose and tongue have a lot to do with taste. [3]Together, they decide if you'd rather have beans or a banana split!

B [4]Your tongue helps create your sense of taste by using its taste buds. [5]Taste buds are those little bumps on your tongue. [6]They are split into four parts on your tongue. [7]The parts are sweet, salt, sour, and bitter. [8]Taste buds notice the taste that is strongest. [9]For example, ice cream has a lot of sugar in it. [10]When you eat ice cream, your taste buds notice a sweet taste. [11]When you eat pizza, they notice sweet and salty tastes.

C [12]Your nose also helps create your sense of taste. [13]Think about the smell of fresh pizza. [14]If you like pizza, the smell excites your sense of taste and can make your mouth water. [15]It smells good, so you want to eat it. [16]What if you have a stuffy nose and can't smell very well? [17]You may not taste things very well either. [18]Have your taste buds stopped working? [19]No. [20]They just don't work as well without your sense of smell.

D [21]Your nose and your tongue are like a team. [22]Each one has a job to do. [23]Each one must do it well to create your sense of taste.

DIRECTIONS: Circle the letter next to the correct answer or write the answer on the lines given. When asked, write the number of the sentence or the letter of the paragraph that is the best evidence.

1. What is the main idea of the story?
   A. Your tongue gives you your sense of taste.
   B. The tip of your tongue tastes sweet things, like ice cream.
   C. The taste buds on your tongue never stop working.
   D. Your nose and tongue create your sense of taste.

   Which 2 sentences are the best evidence? ____, ____

2. What is the main idea of paragraph B?
   A. Your taste buds sense sweet and salty tastes.
   B. Pizza tastes sweet and salty.
   C. Ice cream has lots of sugar in it.
   D. Your tongue uses its taste buds to sense flavors.

   Which sentence is the best evidence? ____

3. Paragraph B supports the main idea of the story by telling about:
   A. your nose and how it works to create your sense of taste.
   B. your tongue and how it works to create your sense of taste.
   C. how ice cream and pizza taste.
   D. taste buds and how they work.

4. What is the main idea of paragraph C?

   _____

   _____

   _____

   Which sentence is the topic sentence? ____

5. Which sentence number below best supports the main idea of paragraph C?
   A. 15
   B. 16
   C. 14
   D. 13

23. The **Wright Stuff** by David White

A [1]Orville and Wilbur Wright invented the airplane in 1903. [2]Orville won a coin toss and got to fly first. [3]On Dec. 17, 1903, he flew 120 feet in 12 seconds.

B [4]The Wrights had been interested in flight since they were boys. [5]They had read all about it. [6]They knew how to build toys and bicycles. [7]Now they were ready to build something they could fly.

C [8]They had built gliders, but these didn't fly very high or far. [9]The challenge was to make something that kept going. [10]The newly invented gasoline engine was their ticket to fly—and keep flying.

D [11]Using a gasoline engine, they flew the plane four times on that day in 1903. [12]Wilbur made the longest flight, which was 852 feet. [13]It took him 59 seconds.

E [14]Orville and Wilbur Wright did a lot in the next few years to make their invention famous. [15]They flew their plane for people all over the country. [16]Wilbur flew around the Statue of Liberty and over New York City. [17]By 1909, the Wrights had formed a business to make and sell their planes. [18]Little did they know how that business would take off.

F [19]Today, airplanes are everywhere. [20]They fly around the world. [21]They fly at night. [22]They fly high in the air. [23]The Wright brothers' ideas live on.

Orville Wright is shown above in the airplane he and his brother designed.

DIRECTIONS: Circle the letter next to the correct answer or write the answer on the lines given. When asked, write the number of the sentence or the letter of the paragraph that is the best evidence.

1. What is the main idea of the story?

   _____

   _____

   _____

2. Which of these sentences is the main idea of paragraph B?
   A. Sentence 4
   B. Sentence 5
   C. Sentence 6
   D. Sentence 7

3. Which of the following sentences would most likely fit in paragraph E?
   A. Airplanes can carry just a few people or more than a hundred.
   B. The gliders also tipped over in the air.
   C. They started in 1900 and kept at it.
   D. Wilbur even went to France to show off the new invention.

4. Which of these sentences is NOT a supporting detail of paragraph E?
   A. Sentence 14
   B. Sentence 15
   C. Sentence 16
   D. Sentence 17

5. Which of these sentences from paragraph F best supports the whole story?
   A. They fly around the world.
   B. They fly high in the air.
   C. The Wright brothers' ideas live on.
   D. Today, airplanes are everywhere.

24. False Face Society by Carrie Beckwith

A ¹The Iroquois Indians thought sickness was caused by bad spirits. ²Sometimes they used medicine to cure sickness. ³Other times, medicine was not enough. ⁴When this happened, they called on the False Face Society.

B ⁵The False Face Society was a secret group of men who were thought to cure sickness. ⁶No one knew who the men were. ⁷When someone was sick, they would do a special dance with masks. ⁸They danced with rattles. ⁹They made noises like "hu, hu, hu." ¹⁰The noises were made to scare away the bad spirits. ¹¹Then one member would rub ashes from the fire over the sick person's head. ¹²Many times they would sing a healing song before they left.

C ¹³Each member of the Society had to make his own mask. ¹⁴He would first find a tree. ¹⁵For three days, he would offer the tree gifts, like tobacco. ¹⁶The Iroquois did this because he wanted to thank the tree for letting him cut into it. ¹⁷After he cut out a piece from the tree, he would take the piece home and work on it.

D ¹⁸There were many types of masks, but some parts of the mask were always the same. ¹⁹For example, they all had big noses and strange mouths. ²⁰Some mouths were twisted or off center. ²¹Some were opened in surprise or closed tight. ²²Masks always had horse hair. ²³The hair could be braided or left hanging down.

E ²⁴Most masks of the False Face Society are in museums. ²⁵However, some Iroquois people still make the masks today.

DIRECTIONS: Circle the letter next to the correct answer or write the answer on the lines given. When asked, write the number of the sentence or the letter of the paragraph that is the best evidence.

1. What is the main idea of the story?
   A. The False Face Society performed with masks to cure the sick.
   B. The False Face Society carved many types of masks.
   C. The masks had healing powers and were needed to keep away evil spirits.
   D. The False Face Society knew how to cure many sicknesses using ashes from a fire.

2. No one knew who the members of the False Face Society were.

   Which 2 sentences are the best evidence? ____, ____

3. What is the main idea of paragraph B? The False Face Society:
   A. wore masks to hide their faces.
   B. danced with rattles.
   C. made noises to scare away the evil spirits.
   D. tried to cure people's sickness.

4. What would a member do with the ashes from the fire?

   _____

   _____

   Which sentence is the best evidence? ____

5. What is the main idea of paragraph D?

   _____

   _____

   Which sentence is the best evidence? ____

6. In paragraph D, which 3 things on the mask were always the same?

   _____

   _____

   Which 2 sentences are the best evidence? ____, ____

IDENTIFYING THEME

Finding the Theme

The theme of a story is the meaning behind the events. A theme presents large issues of human nature such as friendship or courage. Friendship is an important theme in many stories, such as *Charlotte's Web*.

The theme is woven throughout the story. It may be stated directly, or it may be suggested by the characters and events. Authors often show the theme through the characters' actions and words. Remember the fable about the tortoise and the hare? The hare and the tortoise have a race. The hare is a much faster runner, but he plays around during the race. He even stops to take a nap. The tortoise keeps on going, slowly but surely, and wins the race while the hare is napping. What might be a good theme for this fable? "Slow and steady wins the race" or "Never give up" are two possibilities.

When you look for the theme in the story, think about the plot. What problem, or conflict, is presented in the story? How do the characters feel about the problem? What do they do to solve it? Think about the theme for the fable above. What truth is shown by the events in the story? What did the tortoise do that supported the theme?

Now read the following story.

¹Beni loves to watch baseball, but he has used up all his money on this game. ²Now the game is over.

³As he stands up to leave, he finds a wallet on the bench. ⁴It has $10 in it. ⁵That's enough to buy him a ticket to another game! ⁶He could keep the money and leave the wallet. ⁷But that wallet and money belong to someone else. ⁸He would feel guilty. ⁹He looks inside the wallet for a name.

¹⁰"Oliver! Oliver Randall!" he shouts. ¹¹Oliver Randall is down by the exit, but he comes back.

¹²Oliver is surprised to see his wallet. ¹³"I didn't even know I lost it!" he says. ¹⁴"I'm so happy to get it back." ¹⁵He pulls something from his pocket. ¹⁶He says, "I want you to have my extra tickets to the rest of the games."

1. Which of the following is the best theme for this story?
   A. Ballgames are only for the rich.
   B. Sporting events are exciting.
   C. Cheating can get you more tickets.
   D. Honesty is more rewarding than cheating.

What problem is presented in the story? Beni doesn't have enough money to go to more games. Then he finds a wallet with money.

What is Beni's conflict in the story? He has to decide what to do with the money. If he gives the money back, he can't go to another game. If he keeps it, he will feel guilty.

What does Beni do to solve this? He decides to find the owner and give it back.

Which of the choices above are supported by the events in the story? There is no real evidence given in the story to support choice A. Choice B is probably true, but it is not the central idea of the story. Choice C is suggested by sentences 5 and 6, but it is not proven by the rest of the story. Choice D is the best answer. It is supported by Beni's actions in the story and the final result of the story in sentence 16.

25. A Nutty Modern Folktale by David White

A ¹The peanut butter and jam sandwich was an accident. ²It was an accident that helped bring peace to the world.

B ³Many moons ago, the Nutters and the Jammers were mad at each other. ⁴The two groups were not at all alike. ⁵They read different books. ⁶They sang different songs. ⁷They even ate different foods. ⁸One of these foods was the sandwich. ⁹The Nutters ate only peanut butter on bread. ¹⁰The Jammers ate only jam on bread.

C ¹¹A high wall stood between the Nutters and the Jammers. ¹²They each grew their own food. ¹³However, they got their sandwiches from a factory. ¹⁴This factory was built on both sides of the wall. ¹⁵The Nutters spread peanut butter on bread. ¹⁶The Jammers spread jam on bread.

D ¹⁷One day, the factory crumbled. ¹⁸A strong earthquake had shaken the land. ¹⁹Everything on both sides was thrown into a big pile in the middle. ²⁰On top was a bunch of sandwiches. ²¹Mixed together were slices of bread with peanut butter and slices of bread with jam.

E ²²Some workers didn't trust the new sandwich. ²³They didn't think it was right to mix peanut butter with jam. ²⁴Others gave it a try. ²⁵The ones who tried it liked it. ²⁶They told other people. ²⁷Other people tried the new food. ²⁸Word got around. ²⁹Orders for the peanut butter and jelly sandwich poured in.

F ³⁰The workers rebuilt the factory but not the wall. ³¹It was the first step toward peace.

DIRECTIONS: Circle the letter next to the correct answer or write the answer on the lines given. When asked, write the number of the sentence or the letter of the paragraph that is the best evidence.

1. What is the theme of the story?
   A. An accident brings people together.
   B. People can invent great things in times of trouble.
   C. People have different ideas about how to live.
   D. A wall is the best way to separate people.

   Which paragraph is the best evidence? _____

2. Which of these sentences from paragraph B gives the main idea of the paragraph?
   A. The Nutters ate only peanut butter on bread.
   B. The Jammers ate only jam on bread.
   C. The two groups were not at all alike.
   D. They even ate different foods.

3. Look at the following sets of sentences from paragraph B. Which set best supports the idea that the two groups of people liked different types of food?
   A. 3 and 4
   B. 5 and 6
   C. 7 and 8
   D. 9 and 10

4. What is the main idea of paragraph C? The wall:
   A. kept both sides together.
   B. was high enough that nobody could climb over.
   C. kept both sides separate.
   D. was built on both sides of the factory.

5. How does the rest of paragraph D support the main idea—that the factory fell down?

   _____

   _____

   _____

26. Home Away From Earth by Cheryl Block

A   ¹It had been a year since they landed on Mars. ²They lived on the spaceship while the colony was being built. ³The ship was small, and there was no place to play. ⁴Shigai wanted a home, any home.

B   ⁵Sometimes he went with his dad when they left the ship. ⁶Mars was such a strange planet. ⁷The sky was red, not blue. ⁸You had to wear a spacesuit outside. ⁹The air on Mars was mostly carbon dioxide. ¹⁰There wasn't enough oxygen to last more than a few minutes without a spacesuit. ¹¹The colony would be underground to protect them from the planet's surface.

C   ¹²The sandy red soil seemed to suck Shigai down as he walked along. ¹³There were often dust storms on the surface. ¹⁴Work had to stop each time there was a storm.

D   ¹⁵Shigai missed the color green. ¹⁶Since there was no water, nothing grew on the planet's surface. ¹⁷There was nothing on Mars except sand and rocks. ¹⁸What he wouldn't give to see a tree!

E   ¹⁹Some day they would build greenhouses to grow their own food. ²⁰They also hoped to find a way to melt the ice trapped under the surface. ²¹For now, everything had to come on supply ships. ²²They couldn't survive without those ships.

F   ²³"Dust storm!" someone yelled. ²⁴Everyone hurried to the ship. ²⁵The first time a dust storm hit, they lost two men. ²⁶They were never found.

G   ²⁷The huge dust storms were like tornadoes. ²⁸They picked up objects in their path and swirled them around faster and faster. ²⁹Shigai felt the wind pulling him as he stumbled through the thick red dust. ³⁰He could barely see the spaceship in front of him as they climbed aboard.

DIRECTIONS: Circle the letter next to the correct answer or write the answer on the lines given. When asked, write the number of the sentence or the letter of the paragraph that is the best evidence.

1. Which sentence is the topic sentence of paragraph B?

   Sentence _____

2. What is the main idea of paragraph D?
   A. Shigai's favorite color is green.
   B. No green plants grow on Mars.
   C. Shigai misses the green plants from home.
   D. There are only rocks and sand on Mars.

3. Which of the following is the best theme for this story?
   A. Humans can't win against Nature.
   B. There is no place like home.
   C. People must adjust to a new place.
   D. Mars is an unusual planet.

4. Which sentence from paragraph A best supports the idea that Shigai is tired of living on the ship?

   Sentence _____

5. Which sentence from paragraph F best supports the idea that dust storms were dangerous?

   Sentence _____

6. Why was the colony being built underground?

   _____

   _____

   _____

   Which sentence is the best evidence? _____

27. **Giant Hoax** by Margaret Hockett

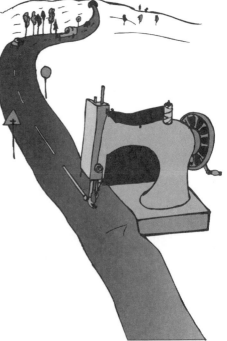

A ¹The Doakers were very small people. ²They knew nothing about the giants. ³That made it easy for the giants to play tricks on them.

B ⁴For example, a Doaker would work and sweat to build a house. ⁵Then a wind (giant's breath!) would come up and blow it down. ⁶Or a Doaker would have to climb over a log that would suddenly rise high in the air. ⁷Road signs would be switched. ⁸Entire trees would disappear!

C ⁹One day, some Doakers climbed a very high mountain and thought wisely. ¹⁰They saw a giant's huge foot as he slept in the broad valley below. ¹¹Then they knew that giants had been causing their troubles. ¹²They made plans.

D ¹³Strange things started happening to the giants. ¹⁴One would take a bite of fruit, only to find that it was hollow! ¹⁵Another would wake up with a beard full of knots. ¹⁶Still another giant would find her fingers glued together.

E ¹⁷But one thing was especially confusing to the giants. ¹⁸The Doakers seemed to be watching even smaller people. (¹⁹Of course, the Doakers were just pretending!) ²⁰It was as if the Doakers were giants themselves! ²¹They blew over tiny houses. ²²They played catch with "invisible" people. ²³And they made little roads that led to nowhere.

F ²⁴When the Doakers weren't around, the giants would get down on the ground. ²⁵They would strain their eyes. ²⁶But, try as they might, the big giants could never see the tiny people. ²⁷It drove them crazy! ²⁸So crazy that they ran far away from Doaker land.

G ²⁹And they have never been seen since.

DIRECTIONS: Circle the letter next to the correct answer or write the answer on the lines given. When asked, write the number of the sentence or the letter of the paragraph that is the best evidence.

1. Paragraph B tells *mainly* about:
   A. how Doakers built their houses.
   B. problems caused by the giants.
   C. Doakers discovering the giants.
   D. how the Doakers lived their lives.

2. What is the theme of the story?
   A. Jokers get what they deserve.
   B. Only giants play tricks.
   C. Life is unfair to little people.
   D. It's hard to stop once you start playing tricks.

   This theme is supported by which paragraph? ____

3. Use paragraph D to list three things the Doakers did to get back at the giants.

   1. _____

   _____

   2. _____

   _____

   3. _____

   _____

4. In paragraph F, which of the following drove the giants crazy?
   A. They were sorry for their tricks.
   B. They ran away from Doaker land.
   C. Their beards and fingers were stuck together.
   D. They couldn't see any tiny people.

   Which 2 sentences from paragraph F are the best evidence? ____, ____

5. In two or three sentences, give a summary of the story.

   _____

   _____

   _____

   _____

   _____

28. *The Cricket in Times Square*
by George Selden (Excerpt)

A   ¹Chester buried his head in the Kleenex. ²He didn't want to see his new friend, Tucker Mouse, get killed. ³Back in Connecticut he had sometimes watched the one-sided fights of cats and mice in the meadow, and unless the mice were near their holes, the fights always ended in the same way. ⁴But this cat had been upon them too quickly: Tucker couldn't have escaped.

B   ⁵There wasn't a sound. ⁶Chester lifted his head and looked very cautiously behind him. ⁷The cat—a huge tiger cat with gray-green and black stripes along his body—was sitting on his hind legs, switching his tail around his forepaws. ⁸And directly between those forepaws, in the very jaws of his enemy, sat Tucker Mouse. ⁹He was watching Chester curiously. ¹⁰The cricket began to make frantic signs that the mouse should look up and see what was looming over him.

C   ¹¹Very casually Tucker raised his head. ¹²The cat looked straight down on him. ¹³"Oh him," said Tucker, chucking the cat under the chin with his right front paw, "he's my best friend. ¹⁴Come out from the matchbox."

D   ¹⁵Chester crept out, looking first at one, then the other.

E   ¹⁶"Chester, meet Harry Cat," said Tucker. ¹⁷"Harry, this is Chester. ¹⁸He's a cricket."

F   ¹⁹"I'm very pleased to make your acquaintance," said Harry Cat in a silky voice.

G   ²⁰"Hello," said Chester. ²¹He was sort of ashamed because of all the fuss he'd made. ²²"I wasn't scared for myself. ²³But I thought cats and mice were enemies."

H   ²⁴"In the country, maybe," said Tucker. ²⁵"But in New York we gave up those old habits long ago. ²⁶Harry is my oldest friend."

DIRECTIONS: Circle the letter next to the correct answer or write the answer on the lines given. When asked, write the number of the sentence or the letter of the paragraph that is the best evidence.

1. What is the main idea of paragraph A?

   A. Chester worries that Tucker won't escape the cat.
   B. The fights between cats and mice in Connecticut are one-sided.
   C. Tucker Mouse is going to be killed.
   D. Tucker Mouse is Chester's new friend.

2. Which paragraph best supports the idea that cats and mice in Connecticut do not get along?

   Paragraph _____

3. Which sentence best shows Harry Cat being friendly?

   Sentence _____

4. What did Chester do to try to warn Tucker of the cat?

   _____

   _____

   _____

   _____

   Which sentence is the best evidence? _____

5. What could be the theme of this passage?

   A. When things get tough, don't give up.
   B. Friends make life more interesting.
   C. Things are not always what they appear to be.
   D. The city is no place for a cricket.

CAUSE AND EFFECT

What is the Cause?

When something happens, you can usually find a reason for it. If you are late for school, the cause may be that you overslept or you missed the bus. When you read a story, you look for the causes of the events in the story. The cause of an event tells you *why* something happened.

Read the following story.

1. [1]Carly had been looking forward to seeing the play. [2]When she arrived at the theater, the sign announced the play was sold out. [3]Since the play was sold out, Carly was not able to see it.

Why wasn't Carly able to see the play? The play was sold out. The word *since* also helps to point out the cause.

It is important to make sure that one event really is the cause of another. While two events can happen at the same time, one event may not have directly caused the other. Read the following story.

2. [1]The cobra is a deadly snake. [2]A cobra will lift its body to attack. [3]Some cobras bite their prey with poisonous fangs. [4]Other cobras squirt the poison in their prey's nose.

What causes the cobra to bite its prey? The answer is not really given in the paragraph. Lifting its body does not cause the cobra to bite. It may lift its body and not attack the prey. Lifting the body and biting may happen together, but one does not actually cause the other.

What is the Effect?

The effect is a change that results from a cause. It tells us *what* happened as a result of something else. For example, "It started to rain on the day of the school picnic, so the picnic was cancelled." The effect was that the picnic was cancelled. The cause was the rain. Usually the cause is given before the effect.

An event can have more than one effect. In the next paragraph, we learn about the effects of the storm before we find out the cause. What were the effects of the storm?

3. [1]Trees were blown down. [2]Streets were flooded. [3]Whole houses were lifted in the air. [4]The damage was **caused by** a tornado that hit our town.

Looking for Signal Words

Certain key words can help you recognize whether an event is a cause or an effect. These words are called signal words.

Signal words that can show **cause**:

because	created by	the reason for	since
caused by	led to	on account of	due to

Signal words that can show **effect**:

therefore	then	as a result	thus
finally	so		

In each of the sentences below, identify the cause and the effect. Look for signal words to help you.

	Cause	Effect
1. **Since** it was getting dark, he went home.	was getting dark	went home
2. A strike by the workers **led to** a safer place to work.	_____	_____
3. They had to stop when their gas **finally** ran out.	_____	_____
4. Jim stayed home **because** he was afraid to fly.	_____	_____
5. Mother wasn't home yet, **so** we couldn't go outside to play.	_____	_____
6. **The reason** Luis was late for class was that he missed the bus.	_____	_____

Recognizing a Series of Causes

Sometimes there can be a sequence of causes for an event. One event causes the next event, which causes the next event, and so on. Look at the story below. What caused the soup to spill?

4.   ¹Tia opened the door suddenly. ²It hit Mr. Cho, and he tripped. ³The bowl went flying out of his hands. ⁴The bowl crashed down. ⁵Soup spilled all over the floor.

In this case, more than one event caused the soup to spill. The door opening caused Mr. Cho to trip. His tripping caused the bowl to fly out of his hands. The soup spilled when the bowl crashed down.

CAUSE AND EFFECT PRACTICE ACTIVITY

Read the following story. Then answer question 1.

¹A young boy fell into the gorilla's exhibit at the zoo. ²The crowd was panicked because the gorilla had picked up the boy! ³As the crowd watched, the gorilla carried the boy to the cage door. ⁴Zookeepers then reached in and pulled the boy out.

1. What caused the crowd to panic?

    _____

    Write the signal word that helped you find the answer.

    _____

Sentence 2 tells you that the crowd panicked because <u>the gorilla picked up the boy</u>. The signal word is ***because***.

Read the next story and answer question 2.

¹Lupe slowly sips Rani's new recipe for soup. ²Her face turns bright red. ³Then her eyes water. ⁴Finally she gasps for air.

⁵"Too much pepper?" asks Rani.

2. What effect does Rani's soup have on Lupe?

    _____

    _____

The soup has several effects on Lupe. Be sure that you wrote all of them.

Which 3 sentences best support the answer? ____, ____, ____

29. High-Rise Doghouse by Margaret Hockett

A ¹Let's say you want a pet. ²So you choose one and build him a simple doghouse! ³You both live happily ever after, right?

B ⁴Wrong. ⁵He'll be really popular. ⁶First, he'll make friends with two strays.

C ⁷The old house will be too crowded, so you'll build a new one. ⁸You'll build a house that is two feet tall (see stage 1).

D ⁹"Whew!" you'll say. ¹⁰"That was hard work." ¹¹But then each dog will find another dog. ¹²There will be two times as many dogs!

E ¹³Back to work. ¹⁴You'll need a house that is twice as tall. ¹⁵The new one will be four feet tall (see stage 2).

F ¹⁶What if each dog asks a relative to move in? ¹⁷Doggone! ¹⁸You'll need to make a high rise (see stage 3).

G ¹⁹Will the building ever end? ²⁰Yes. ²¹It will end when there are too many dogs having too much fun in a too tall house. ²²It will wobble and sway! (²³See stage 4.) ²⁴The dogs will be scared and run away.

H ²⁵Then each dog will find an eager new owner. ²⁶And each new owner will build a doghouse. ²⁷A simple one, first.

Stage 1

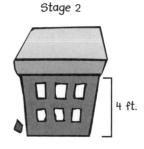
2 ft.

Stage 2

4 ft.

Stage 3

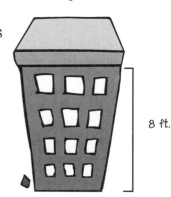
8 ft.

Stage 4

DIRECTIONS: Circle the letter next to the correct answer or write the answer on the lines given. When asked, write the number of the sentence or the letter of the paragraph that is the best evidence.

1. In paragraph C, what will cause you to build a new house?

    _____

    _____

    Which sentence is the best evidence? _____

2a. What results every time more dogs come to live in the doghouse?

    A. Dogs share windows.
    B. The roof is replaced.
    C. The house becomes wider.
    D. The house height doubles.

2b. How do the pictures help you to prove your answer?

    _____

    _____

    _____

3. By the end of paragraph D, we can tell there will be six dogs. How do we know?

    _____

    _____

    _____

    _____

4. What will cause you to make a high-rise doghouse?

    _____

    _____

    Which paragraph is the best evidence? _____

5. Too many dogs have too much fun in a too tall house. Which of the following will probably NOT be a result?

    A. You will build again.
    B. The house will sway.
    C. The dogs will be afraid.
    D. The dogs will run away.

    Which paragraph is the best evidence? _____

30. Cat and Mouse by Cheryl Block

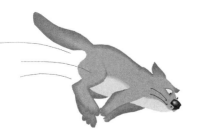

A ¹The little mouse scurried through a hole in the fence. ²The old tom-cat was close behind. ³Since he couldn't fit through the hole, he jumped over the fence. ⁴The mouse ran under a stack of boxes. ⁵The cat reached under the boxes with his paw. ⁶Down came the boxes. ⁷The cat jumped back just in time. ⁸The little mouse ran out.

B ⁹An empty glass jar was lying on the ground. ¹⁰The little mouse quickly squeezed into the jar. ¹¹The cat pounced on it. ¹²The jar spun around and hit him in the nose. ¹³While the cat was rubbing his nose, the mouse ran out of the jar.

C ¹⁴The mouse climbed onto the end of a board that was leaning up against a box. ¹⁵The cat jumped on the other end of the board. ¹⁶Up went the mouse. ¹⁷He flew through the air and landed in a trash can. ¹⁸The cat jumped into the trash can and tipped it over. ¹⁹While the cat climbed out from under the trash, the little mouse quietly scurried away.

DIRECTIONS: Circle the letter next to the correct answer or write the answer on the lines given. When asked, write the number of the sentence or the letter of the paragraph that is the best evidence.

1. In sentence 3, why didn't the cat go through the hole?

   _____

   _____

   Write the signal word from sentence 3.

   _____

2. What caused the cat to jump back in sentence 7?

   _____

   _____

   Which other sentence is the best evidence? _____

3. Why was the cat rubbing his nose in sentence 13?

   A. His nose itched.
   B. The mouse ran away.
   C. The jar hit him.
   D. The board hit him.

   Which sentence is the best evidence? _____

4. What was the result when the cat tipped over the trash can?

   A. The trash can was dented.
   B. The cat jumped into the can.
   C. The cat got hurt.
   D. The cat was covered with trash.

   Which sentence is the best evidence? _____

31. **Streetball Hero** by Carrie Beckwith

A   ¹The street lights were starting to flicker since it was getting dark. ²Ty's mom was calling for him, but he couldn't leave. ³It was the last inning. ⁴He had two balls and one strike. ⁵The bases were empty, and the score was tied.

B   ⁶Ty spit into his hands. ⁷Then he rubbed them around the rubber grip so they were good and tight. ⁸Ameko could pitch faster than anyone in the fifth grade, so Ty was a little nervous. ⁹The crowd was growing loud. ¹⁰"Hey batter, batter, batter," they chanted. ¹¹"Hey, batter, batter, batter... swing!" ¹²Ameko pitched. ¹³Ty swung, but too soon. ¹⁴The ball landed with a loud thump in the catcher's glove.

C   ¹⁵"Strike two!" shouted Ramon, the catcher. ¹⁶Ty moved back into batting position. ¹⁷The chanting started again. ¹⁸"Hey batter, batter, batter..." ¹⁹His face stiffened, but the noise wouldn't cause him to miss this time. ²⁰Ameko pitched the ball.

D   ²¹"Pop!" ²²It flew straight up the side of the telephone pole. ²³"Catch it, Ameko! ²⁴He's out!" the kids on the street curb shouted. ²⁵Ameko held her glove up to the night sky. ²⁶But she couldn't see the ball. ²⁷Finally, it landed—right on the curb! ²⁸Ty flew to first, then second, then third base. ²⁹Ameko picked up the ball and threw it home. ³⁰The shortstop caught the ball. ³¹But Ty was making his way home. ³²He skidded across the street. ³³"He's in, he's in!" Ty's team cheered.

E   ³⁴Ty's team picked him up and carried him home. ³⁵"Hey, Mom!" they shouted from across the street, "You have a winner here!"

DIRECTIONS: Circle the letter next to the correct answer or write the answer on the lines given. When asked, write the number of the sentence or the letter of the paragraph that is the best evidence.

1. Why were the street lights flickering?

   _____

   _____

   _____

   What is the signal word in sentence 1?

   _____

2. Why did Ty stay outside even though his mom was calling for him?

   _____

   _____

   _____

   Which 3 sentences are the best evidence? ____, ____, ____

3. Ty was a little nervous because:
   A. he didn't want to skid on the street.
   B. his mom was calling for him.
   C. the pitcher was really good.
   D. the crowd was growing loud.

   Which sentence is the best evidence? ____

4. What caused Ty to swing and miss?
   A. the noise
   B. Ameko's pitch
   C. the darkness
   D. his nerves

   Which sentence is the best evidence? ____

5. What happened as a result of Ty skidding across the street?

   _____

   _____

   _____

   Which sentence is the best evidence? ____

6. What caused Ameko to miss the ball?

   _____

   _____

   _____

   Which sentence is the best evidence? ____

32. **Northern Lights** by Margaret Hockett

A [1]You look up. [2]A giant curtain of light flickers and waves. [3]Green and red fingers seem to tickle the sky. [4]Huge bands shimmer and ripple. [5]Beams glow and wave. [6]They are like searchlights trying to find you. [7]Their size makes you feel small.

B [8]Are you watching fireworks? [9]No. [10]Are you seeing a laser light show? [11]No. [12]What you see is the result of a natural show. [13]It is called the Northern Lights.

C [14]What causes the Northern Lights? [15]The reason begins in the sun. [16]Storms in the sun cause explosions. [17]Tiny fragments from these explosions are sent to Earth. [18]Earth is like a big magnet, so the North Pole catches some of them. [19]When these fragments come through the air, they cause the air to glow. [20]The air conditions make the light move in different patterns.

D [21]Who can see the Northern Lights? [22]People who live as far north as Canada or the northern United States may see them.

E [23]When can these lights be seen? [24]No one knows exactly. [25]It may depend on the sun's activities and Earth's air conditions. [26]Whenever the lights are seen, though, they create joy for many people.

DIRECTIONS: Circle the letter next to the correct answer or write the answer on the lines given. When asked, write the number of the sentence or the letter of the paragraph that is the best evidence.

1. Paragraph A suggests that you feel small because

   A. the bands are so big.
   B. the fingers are huge.
   C. the searchlights move.
   D. you are looking upward.

   Which sentence is the best evidence? _____

2. The sights in paragraph A are a result of:

   A. a fireworks display.
   B. a laser show.
   C. a natural show.
   D. searchlights.

   Which sentence is the best evidence? _____

3. The Northern Lights are NOT a result of:

   A. the sun's storms.
   B. Earth's being like a magnet.
   C. bands waving in the air.
   D. bits from the sun.

   Which paragraph is the best evidence? _____

4. Why does the air near the North Pole trap the fragments from the sun?

   A. The air is thick.
   B. Earth is like a magnet.
   C. The air is clean.
   D. The pole is close to the sun.

   Which sentence is the best evidence? _____

5. In each sentence below, underline the cause and circle the effect.

   1. When these fragments come through the air, they cause the air to glow.

   2. The air conditions make the light move in different patterns.

6. According to paragraph E, what happens when the Northern Lights are seen?

   _____

   _____

   Which sentence is the best evidence? _____

33. Space Chase by Carrie Beckwith

A ¹It sounded like the booming of a giant drum. ²"What's that noise?" Jade asked.

B ³"It's a space jet!" Vi cried as the jet sped by.

C ⁴"Did you see it?" Jade asked.

D ⁵"It went by so fast! ⁶All I saw was a flash of light."

E ⁷The girls were moving closer to the front of the line. ⁸Soon they, too, would be flying in "The Space Zone."

F ⁹The voice of a jet pilot sounded from above. ¹⁰It was filled with panic. ¹¹"Starship 104, this is Galaxy Cruiser 571. ¹²You have an enemy jet on your right wing! ¹³Drop down now before you're hit!"

G ¹⁴The radio made a hissing sound, then cut off. ¹⁵Lasers darted across the blackness. ¹⁶The Starship dropped then flipped on its side. ¹⁷The firing followed its path. ¹⁸The voice of the jet pilot sounded again.

H ¹⁹"I'm moving behind him, Starship. ²⁰Keep him on your tail a little longer." ²¹The Galaxy jet pilot zoomed in. ²²"Center it. ²³Easy now," he whispered to himself. ²⁴"Shoot!" ²⁵Streams of lasers fired from the Galaxy Cruiser. ²⁶The jet was hit. ²⁷Slowly, the enemy jet glided down to the landing where Vi and Jade waited.

I ²⁸"Look, Vi, there's the enemy pilot. ²⁹It's finally our turn to ride the jet." ³⁰The pilot climbed out of the small ship. ³¹His face broke into a grin. ³²"That was the best ride of my life! ³³I'm doing it again."

J ³⁴"You'll have to wait in line for the next ride," Vi kidded. ³⁵"This jet is ready for *real* pilots now!"

DIRECTIONS: Circle the letter next to the correct answer or write the answer on the lines given. When asked, write the number of the sentence or the letter of the paragraph that is the best evidence.

1. What caused the loud noise Jade and Vi heard?

   _____

   _____

   Which sentence is the best evidence?____

2. Why was it hard for Vi to see the jet?

   _____

   _____

   Which sentence is the best evidence? ____

3. What caused the Galaxy Cruiser pilot to panic?
   A. He saw the Galaxy Cruiser behind him.
   B. He saw the Starship start to drop.
   C. He saw the Starship flip on its side.
   D. He thought the enemy jet would hit the Starship.

   Which 2 sentences are the best evidence? ____, ____

4. What caused the enemy jet to come down?

   _____

   _____

   _____

   Which 2 sentences are the best evidence? ____, ____

5. Why were the girls waiting on the landing?
   A. They were waiting for a friend to get off the ride.
   B. They wanted to ride on the jet.
   C. They wanted to get a better view of the enemy pilot.
   D. They were forced to move there.

   Which 2 sentences are the best evidence? ____, ____

34. The Secret of Popcorn by David White

A [1]How does popcorn pop? [2]Water is the key. [3]A kernel of popcorn is about 13 percent water. [4]This water is in a layer of soft starch. [5]An outer layer made of a hard starch surrounds the inner layer. [6]Heating the popcorn causes the water to turn into steam. [7]This is why your popcorn is not wet. [8]The inner layer heats more quickly than the outer layer. [9]The steam pushes the outer layer. [10]Finally, when the steam pressure is too much, pop! [11]The kernel turns inside out. [12]Out pops the soft, white starch.

B [13]More fun facts:

- [14]A kernel that loses 3 percent of its water will not pop.

- [15]One cup of unpopped popcorn can make 30 cups of popped corn.

- [16]Popcorn must be heated to 400°F for it to pop.

- [17]One of the first uses for the microwave oven was to pop popcorn.

DIRECTIONS: Circle the letter next to the correct answer or write the answer on the lines given. When asked, write the number of the sentence or the letter of the paragraph that is the best evidence.

1. Number the following events in order that cause a kernel to pop.

    ____ The starch pops out.
    ____ The kernel turns inside out.
    ____ The heat turns the water layer to steam.
    ____ The pressure pushes the outer layer.

2. What causes the water to turn into steam?

    A. water
    B. starch
    C. heat
    D. pressure

    Which sentence is the best evidence? ____

3. What two things mentioned in the story could keep a kernel from popping?

    1. _____

    _____

    2. _____

    _____

    Which 2 sentences are the best evidence?____, ____

4. What would happen if you heated popcorn kernels to 350°? The popcorn would be:

    A. stuck together.
    B. white and fluffy.
    C. hard kernels.
    D. corn on the cob.

    Which sentence is the best evidence? ____

35. "Tracks" From *The Stories Huey Tells*
by Ann Cameron (Excerpt)

A ¹The next night I woke up. ²I looked at the clock that sits on top of the brick on my night table. ³It was 1 a.m.

B ⁴Julian was asleep with his pillow over his head. ⁵I went down to the living room.

C ⁶I found his book on top of the TV, open to a page on African safaris. ⁷I went down to the basement and got my dad's hammer. ⁸I took it and the book outside. ⁹The moon was not quite as big as the night before, but there was plenty of light for working.

D ¹⁰Every few feet I mashed up small spots of sandy ground with the hammer. ¹¹Then I rounded them out just right.

E ¹²I stood up and compared them to the picture in Julian's book. ¹³They looked the way they were supposed to—just like zebra tracks. ¹⁴Zebras leave hoofprints like horses. ¹⁵Their tracks are deeper in the ground than raccoon tracks. ¹⁶That's why I used the hammer.

F ¹⁷In the morning, Julian was so excited he was yelling.

G ¹⁸"Mom and Dad! ¹⁹Huey! ²⁰Come look! ²¹There was a *zebra* here last night!"

H ²²We all ran outside. ²³My dad studied Julian's book and the tracks.

I ²⁴"Hard to believe," my dad said, "but it sure does look that way!"

DIRECTIONS: Circle the letter next to the correct answer or write the answer on the lines given. When asked, write the number of the sentence or the letter of the paragraph that is the best evidence.

1. Why did Huey go down to the basement?

   A. to find Julian's book
   B. to get the hammer
   C. to check the clock
   D. to find a flashlight

   Which sentence is the best evidence? ____

2. Why did Huey use a hammer to make the prints?

   _____

   _____

   Which 2 sentences are the best evidence? ____, ____

3. In paragraph C, how was Huey able to see as he worked?

   _____

   _____

   Which sentence is the best evidence? ____

4. Why was Julian excited?

   _____

   _____

   Which sentence is the best evidence?____

5. What made Huey's dad believe that these were zebra tracks?

   A. He matched them with Julian's book.
   B. He saw the zebra.
   C. He looked at them.
   D. He carefully measured them with a ruler.

   Which sentence is the best evidence? ____

MAKING PREDICTIONS

Making Predictions

A good reader is always making predictions about what will happen next in a story. A prediction is really a guess that you make using as much information as possible. The more information you have, the more likely your prediction will be true. When you try to predict how someone is going to act, you base your prediction on that character's traits and past actions. How has he or she behaved in the past? What will this character probably do this time? Read the following passage.

1. [1]Uncle George was a huge man. [2]He was so big he was almost scary. [3]But he was the kindest soul I ever knew. [4]He was always helping people. [5]If someone needed a hand, he could count on Uncle George. [6]He had never said no to anyone.

What would Uncle George do if a neighbor asked him for a favor?

Predicting Outcomes

When you predict the ending, or outcome, of a story, you should base your predictions on what has happened so far in the story. What do you already know about the characters from the story? Focus on the characters' traits and actions. Will their behavior change? All of this is evidence that you can use to support your prediction. Read the following passage. Can you predict what Gloria will do?

2. [1]Gloria climbed the steps slowly. [2]She didn't want to try the ride. [3]It was too high, it was too fast, it was too scary. [4]Eddie said she was being a baby, but she didn't care. [5]She just didn't like roller coasters. [6]She hadn't been on one yet. [7]She let the people behind her go in front. [8]Just watching the cars go up and down was making her dizzy. [9]That made up her mind.

Your prediction will likely be based on how much evidence you have to support it. We know that Gloria doesn't like roller coasters and doesn't want to ride this one. She hasn't ridden one yet. Since she let the people behind her go ahead, she probably isn't going to ride this one either.

PREDICTION PRACTICE ACTIVITY

Activity 1

Read the first four sentences of the story. Then answer the question.

¹Merill loved eating lunch outside with Randy. ²They always ate lunch outside in fair weather. ³They even ate out there if it was windy. ⁴They ate out there if it was cloudy or foggy or snowy.

1. Where do you predict they will eat if today is sunny?

   _____

   Which sentence is the best evidence? _____

Activity 2

Read the rest of the story. Then answer the questions.

⁵There were only three days they had not eaten outdoors. ⁶On September 30, it sprinkled. ⁷On October 15 and 16, it poured. ⁸Randy did not like to get wet. ⁹Today, she was packing her lunch cheerfully when she heard something on the roof. ¹⁰She frowned as the pitter-patter grew louder.

2. What do you think the weather will be like today?

   _____

   Which 2 sentences are the best evidence? ____, ____

3. Where do you predict they will eat today?

   _____

36. Missing Ring by David White

A   [1]"Isn't it great?" Sam asked. [2]He handed it to his friend Jose. [3]It was a secret code ring. [4]Inside was a small wheel, which you turned to reveal different symbols. [5]Sam had the code book. [6]As Jose turned the wheel, Sam told him what the symbols meant. [7]After three turns, the boys went back to eating. [8]The lunchroom was loud. [9]Jose set the ring down by his lunch plate.

B   [10]The next thing they knew, the ring was gone. [11]"I looked away for five seconds," Jose said. [12]"I thought I heard someone call my name." [13]He hung his head. [14]"I need to be more careful."

C   [15]Bruiser Flynn and his friends laughed as they walked by, heading toward the door. [16]Pudge Sanders put a donut in his jacket pocket.

D   [17]"Pudge, you full?" Bruiser asked. [18]"I've never seen you save anything for later." [19]Pudge kept walking.

E   [20]"Detective" Darla had overheard Bruiser talking. [21]She hadn't been looking at the boys when the ring vanished. [22]She was on the case now.

F   [23]She watched Pudge shuffle out, keeping his hands in his pockets. [24]She saw part of the donut peeking out of his jacket. [25]She saw Pudge look quickly at Sam and Jose.

G   [26]"How big is that ring?" she asked.

H   [27]"Big as a fingertip," Sam replied.

I   [28]"Well," Darla said, clapping her hands, "I know the 'hole' truth."

DIRECTIONS: Circle the letter next to the correct answer or write the answer on the lines given. When asked, write the number of the sentence or the letter of the paragraph that is the best evidence.

1. Where do you predict the ring will be found?

   A. in a trash can
   B. in a donut hole
   C. in the food line
   D. in the kitchen

   Which 3 sentences are the best evidence? ____, ____, ____

2a. What would probably happen if Pudge tried to read the symbols in the code ring?

   _____

   _____

   _____

2b. Why?

   _____

   _____

   Which paragraph is the best evidence? ____

3. What will Jose probably do next time someone hands him something important?

   _____

   _____

   Which sentence is the best evidence? ____

4. What will Darla probably tell Sam she saw? List two things.

   1. _____

   _____

   2. _____

   _____

   Which paragraph is the best evidence? ____

37. The City Street Game by David White

A   [1]Jenny is new to Baker Street and wants to join the Baker Street Club. [2]Carlos, her neighbor, says she has to prove herself by passing a test.

B   [3]"First, you have to run from Tree 1 to Tree 2," he explains, pointing at the two trees.

C   [4]Jenny looks where he points. [5]Tree 1 is at her end of the street, and Tree 2 is at the other end. [6]"That's easy enough," says Jenny as she starts down the street.

D   [7]"Wait, that's not all!" says Carlos. [8]"On the way to Tree 2, you have to say your name each time you pass a house."

E   [9]"Got it. [10]Jenny!" she shouts as she starts again and passes in front of a house.

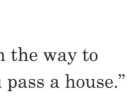

F   [11]"Hold on!" says Imelda. [12]"You also have to run around both fire hydrants, first the red then the yellow. [13]If you hear any of us yell 'Stop!' you have to freeze until we say 'Go.'"

G   [14]"Is that all?" Jenny asks. [15]This is harder than she thought, but she's not worried.

H   [16]"There is one more thing," Carlos says. [17]"You have to follow all the rules. [18]You are given one chance to start over if you don't follow a rule. [19]If you make two mistakes, you fail the test!"

I   [20]There are a lot of rules, but Jenny knows she can remember them. [21]After all, she was always the first on her old street to understand new games.

J   [22]She starts running toward Tree 2.

DIRECTIONS: Circle the letter next to the correct answer or write the answer on the lines given. When asked, write the number of the sentence or the letter of the paragraph that is the best evidence.

1. Predict what would happen if Jenny ran around the yellow fire hydrant before she ran around the red fire hydrant.

   A. She would hear the word "Stop!"
   B. She would have to run back to Tree 1.
   C. She would say her name.
   D. She would have to wait until she heard "Go."

   Which sentence is the best evidence? _____

2. What would probably happen if Jenny heard the word "Stop" while she was passing a house?

   A. She would fail the test.
   B. She would stop moving.
   C. She would start over.
   D. She would say her name.

   Which sentence is the best evidence? _____

3. Predict what could happen if no one yelled the word "Stop" during Jenny's game.

   _____

   _____

   _____

4. Does Jenny have a good chance of passing the test? Explain your answer.

   _____

   _____

   _____

   Which 2 sentences are the best evidence? _____, _____

38. Real Pirates by Margaret Hockett

A   [1]BaBoom! [2]Cannon smoke fills the air. [3]The villagers fire muskets toward the ship. [4]Will that scare off the invaders? [5]Hardly! [6]The pirates take over our town on the St. Lawrence River. [7]The mayor hands them the keys to Alexandria Bay. [8]But she's smiling! [9]It was a great show, and it happens every year.

B   [10]Pirate Days is fun. [11]But I overhear some men planning to rob the ticket booth. [12]They wear pirate clothes and fit right into the crowd.

Come One, Come All, to Pirate Days!

C   [13]The short one waves a musket in the air. [14]He says, "Gimme your money, landlubbers!" [15]He runs up to the ticket booth. [16]Two of his men draw their swords. [17]Two others tie up the cops standing nearby. [18]Everyone is laughing and clapping. [19]They think it's another show!

D   [20]Shorty grabs Ruth, the ticket lady. [21]He makes her open the cash box. [22]Her eyes grow large with fear. [23]"Help! Robbers!" she hollers. [24]Everyone thinks Ruth is a good actor. [25]Shorty stuffs a sock in her mouth.

E   [26]I run to the cops. [27]Shorty and his men run off with the cash.

F   [28]"Stop them! [29]They're real pirates!" I yell.

G   [30]"Sure, Honey, we'll throw 'em in jail!" one says as he unties the rope. [31]Everyone looks at me and laughs.

H   [32]How can I make them believe a girl my age?

DIRECTIONS: Circle the letter next to the correct answer or write the answer on the lines given. When asked, write the number of the sentence or the letter of the paragraph that is the best evidence.

1. Based on paragraph A, predict how the people would feel if the pirates did NOT invade the town.
   A. disappointed
   B. tired
   C. pleased
   D. satisfied

2. What would a tourist probably do if she saw someone dressed as a pirate robbing someone on the street during Pirate Days?
   A. stop him
   B. call the police
   C. pay no attention
   D. watch him

   Which 2 sentences from paragraph C are the best evidence?_____, _____

3. Let's say one of the robbers from the story wanted to rob people at the circus. How would he probably dress?
   A. as a gang member
   B. as a clown
   C. as a pirate
   D. as a robber

   Which paragraph is the best evidence? _____

4. What would Ruth probably do if there were no sock in her mouth?
   A. take a bow
   B. pretend to be mad
   C. say nothing
   D. yell for help

   Which sentence from paragraph D is the best evidence? _____

5. Based on paragraph H, predict what the girl will do next.
   A. take the sock from Ruth's mouth
   B. give up and go home
   C. untie the cops
   D. just watch the parade as it passes

39. Pinch, Pull, Coil by Cheryl Block

A   [1]People have been making pots for a long time. [2]With a little practice and some clay, you can make a pot. [3]Two of the easiest pots to make are the pinch pot and the coil pot.

pinch pot

B   [4]You make a pinch pot by squeezing the clay with your fingers. [5]Start with a ball of clay. [6]Press your thumb into the ball to make a dent in the middle. [7]Don't go all the way through the clay!

C   [8]Next, gently squeeze the sides of the pot between your thumb and fingers while you turn the pot. [9]Turning the pot helps to keep the sides even as you make them thinner. [10]You should always work from the bottom of the pot out towards the edges.

D   [11]The coil pot can be used to make lots of interesting bowls and vases. [12]A coil pot is made by rolling out long "snakes" of clay. [13]These snakes are curled into coils, or rings, and the coils are stacked on top of each other.

E   [14]First roll out a flat slab of clay and cut out a circle to make a base for the pot. [15]Now roll out several clay snakes. [16]Be sure to roll the clay gently from the center out so it doesn't break. [17]Coil the snake around the edge of the base. [18]Stick it on with a paste made of clay and water. [19]Then cut the coil so the ends meet. [20]Press the coils together inside and outside until you have a solid wall. [21]Keep adding coils with the paste and pressing them together until the pot is the height you want.

F   [22]You can make different shapes when you stack the coils. [23]Put the coils directly one on top of the other to make a cylinder. [24]You can change the shape of the pot by overlapping the edges of the coils as you stack them.

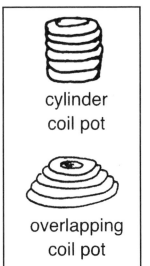

cylinder
coil pot

overlapping
coil pot

G   [25]The last step in making either a pinch pot or a coil pot is to bake it. [26]Baking will make the pot hard. [27]Wait about a week until the pot is dry before you bake it.

DIRECTIONS: Circle the letter next to the correct answer or write the answer on the lines given. When asked, write the number of the sentence or the letter of the paragraph that is the best evidence.

1. In paragraph C, what might your pot look like if you didn't turn it?
   A. The sides could stay thick all around.
   B. The sides could be uneven.
   C. There would be no difference.
   D. The sides could be thin all around.

   Which sentence is the best evidence? _____

2. Based on the pictures, how will the shape change if you overlap the coils?

   _____

   _____

   Which paragraph is the best evidence? _____

3. In paragraph E, what could happen if you roll the coil from the outside ends to the center?

   _____

   Which sentence is the best evidence? _____

4. In paragraph E, what might happen if you forget to press the coils on the inside?
   A. You wouldn't have a solid wall inside.
   B. The coils would stick together.
   C. You couldn't cut the ends of the coils.
   D. You couldn't add more coils.

   Which sentence is the best evidence? _____

5. What could happen if you didn't bake your pot?

   _____

   _____

   Which sentence is the best evidence? _____

40. Eddy the Bully by Carrie Beckwith

A [1]Rosy started the whole thing. [2]She told Eddy, the meanest kid in school, that I was talking about him. [3]Sure enough, he walked up to me at recess. [4]It was just like he did to that poor kid last week.

B [5]"Have you been talking about me, little guy?" he asked with a smile. [6]Eddy liked to ask a few questions before he got into it. [7]You didn't want to get funny with him. [8]He'd already been kicked out of two schools for fighting.

C [9]"I...I've never said anything about you, Eddy," I tried to explain. [10]I could have written an essay on why I would never say anything bad about Eddy. [11]I wasn't a fighter. [12]I was a thinker. [13]And I had a good head I wanted to protect. [14]But it was useless. [15]Eddy moved in closer. [16]His warm breath smelled like rotten milk. [17]Then Rosy showed up.

D [18]"Hey, Josh. [19]What's the matter? [20]You look a little scared," she teased.

E [21]We were drawing a crowd now. [22]Kids quit playing ball to come over and watch us. [23]I imagined myself becoming a memory. *[24]What would Mom and Dad do without me? [25]Who would feed my goldfish?* [26]Seconds felt like hours. [27]Then the bell rang. [28]The crowd started to break up. *[29]Why were they walking away?* I wondered. [30]The recess bell never stopped anyone from watching a good fight. [31]It was like standing up and leaving a movie right before the best part.

F [32]Then I saw her. [33]A tall woman with a whistle around her neck was coming towards us. [34]It was Mrs. Hicks—the principal.

DIRECTIONS: Circle the letter next to the correct answer or write the answer on the lines given. When asked, write the number of the sentence or the letter of the paragraph that is the best evidence.

1. Besides Eddy and Josh, who else might get into trouble with the principal? Explain why.

    _____

    _____

    _____

    _____

    Which 2 sentences are the best evidence? ____, ____

2. What do you think will happen to Eddy if he doesn't quit fighting?

    _____

    _____

    Which sentence is the best evidence? ____

3. What do you think would have happened if Mrs. Hicks had not shown up?

    _____

    _____

    Which sentence from paragraph E is the best evidence? ____

4. If Eddy got into a fight with someone at your school, what would he probably do before he started to fight?

    _____

    _____

    _____

    Which sentence is the best evidence? ____

5. Do you think Josh would fight if a smaller kid picked a fight with him? Explain your answer.

    _____

    _____

    _____

    _____

    Which 3 sentences are the best evidence? ____, ____, ____

41. **How Lies Are Detected** by Margaret Hockett

A [1]Have you ever told a lie? [2]When you lie, you may look and sound honest. [3]People may believe your words. [4]But they won't see your hands sweat. [5]They won't hear you breathing faster. [6]They won't notice your faster heartbeat or your rising blood pressure.

B [7]A lie detector is a machine that notices these four body responses. [8]Tools called sensors are used to measure each response. [9]Clips are put on your fingers. [10]A sleeve is wrapped around your arm to take your blood pressure. [11]A band surrounds your chest. [12]Each of these sensors is connected to a pen that draws patterns of waves to create a chart. [13]The patterns show your hand sweat response, your heart rate, your blood pressure, and your breathing pattern.

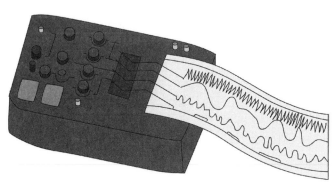

C [14]What happens during a lie detector test? [15]First, you must answer simple questions with a yes or no. [16]The tester may state your name and ask if that is your name. [17]You must answer one time with a *yes* and another time with a *no*. [18]The chart will show how you respond when you lie and when you tell the truth. [19]Then you must answer the important questions. [20]When an expert reads the chart, he or she will decide if your responses show lies or truth.

D [21]You cannot always trust the results of a lie detector because some people can fool the machine. [22]Even so, the lie detector may still be used to discover the truth about crimes.

DIRECTIONS: Circle the letter next to the correct answer or write the answer on the lines given. When asked, write the number of the sentence or the letter of the paragraph that is the best evidence.

1. Let's say your friend earned an F but lied and said he got an A. As he lied, what would probably happen to his heart rate? It would:

   A. slow down.
   B. speed up.
   C. stay the same.
   D. disappear.

   Which sentence is the best evidence? ____

2. What would happen if the pens were removed before your lie detector test?

   A. No chart would be made.
   B. You would have no heart beat.
   C. The waves would increase.
   D. You would be called a liar.

   Which sentence is the best evidence? ____

3. If someone gave you a lie detector test but didn't care about your hand sweat response, he might leave off:

   A. the pens.
   B. the chart.
   C. a finger clip.
   D. an arm sleeve.

   Which paragraph is the best evidence? ____

4. Rob Banks is accused of stealing money. He takes a lie detector test. Which question will he most likely be asked first?

   A. Did you steal the money?
   B. Where were you during the robbery?
   C. Is your name Rob Banks?
   D. What kind of pizza do you like?

   Which 2 sentences are the best evidence? ____, ____

5. You answer all the questions on a lie detector test. Two of your "yes" responses make wave patterns different from your normal truth pattern. What will the test reader think?

   Which paragraph is the best evidence? ____

42. *Sideways Stories From Wayside School*
by Louis Sachar (Excerpt)

A   [1]Joe counted the potatoes. [2]"Seven, five, three, one, two, four, six, eight. [3]There are eight potatoes, Mrs. Jewls."

B   [4]"No, there are eight," said Mrs. Jewls.

C   [5]"But that's what I said," said Joe. [6]"May I go to recess now?"

D   [7]"No, you got the right answer, but you counted the wrong way again." [8]She put three books on his desk. [9]"Count the books, Joe."

E   [10]Joe counted the books. [11]"A thousand, a million, three. [12]Three, Mrs. Jewls."

F   [13]"Correct," said Mrs. Jewls.

G   [14]"May I go to recess now?" Joe asked.

H   [15]"No," said Mrs. Jewls.

I   [16]"May I have a potato?" asked Joe.

J   [17]"No, listen to me. [18]One, two, three, four, five, six, seven, eight, nine, ten," said Mrs. Jewls. [19]"Now you say it."

K   [20]"One, two, three, four, five, six, seven, eight, nine, ten," said Joe.

L   [21]"Very good!" said Mrs. Jewls. [22]She put six erasers on his desk. [23]"Now count the erasers, Joe, just the way I showed you."

M   [24]Joe counted the erasers. [25]"One, two, three, four, five, six, seven, eight, nine, ten. [26]There are ten, Mrs. Jewls."

N   [27]"No," said Mrs. Jewls.

O   [28]"This doesn't make any sense," said Joe. [29]"When I count the wrong way I get the right answer, and when I count right I get the wrong answer."

P   [30]Mrs. Jewls hit her head against the wall five times. [31]"How many times did I hit my head against the wall?" she asked.

Q   [32]"One, two, three, four, five, six, seven, eight, nine, ten. [33]You hit your head against the wall ten times," said Joe.

R   [34]"No," said Mrs. Jewls.

S   [35]"Four, six, one, nine, five. [36]You hit your head five times," said Joe.

T   [37]Mrs. Jewls shook her head no and said, "Yes, that is right."

DIRECTIONS: Circle the letter next to the correct answer or write the answer on the lines given. When asked, write the number of the sentence or the letter of the paragraph that is the best evidence.

1. Let's say Mrs. Jewls gives Joe nine bananas. She tells him to count like she showed him in paragraph J. How many bananas will Joe say there are?

   A. ten
   B. nine
   C. five
   D. none

2. Let's say Joe is given seven oranges. He is asked to tell how many there are. What does he say?

   _____

   _____

   Which 3 paragraphs are the best evidence? _____, _____, _____

3. What would happen if Joe were to count correctly *and* get the right answer? Mrs. Jewls would:

   A. say he counted wrong.
   B. say he got the wrong answer.
   C. let him go to recess.
   D. keep him inside to do math.

   Which 2 sentences from paragraphs C and D are the best evidence? _____, _____

4. Let's say Mrs. Jewls shows Joe eleven marbles. What two possible answers might he give?

   _____

   _____

   Explain your answer.

   _____

   _____

   _____

   _____

5. Paragraphs C and D show how Mrs. Jewls helps Joe with counting. What would Mrs. Jewls probably do if a student had trouble with her alphabet letters? Mrs. Jewls would:

   A. not do anything.
   B. punish her later.
   C. send a book home.
   D. help her at school.

43. Down the Drain by Cheryl Block

A ¹I tried to climb up the sides. ²I kept sliding back down. ³There had to be some way to get out of this sink.

B ⁴Dad came in. ⁵He would help me. ⁶I yelled and yelled. ⁷Dad didn't hear me. ⁸I already knew he couldn't see me without his glasses.

C ⁹Oh no! ¹⁰Dad was going to brush his teeth! ¹¹I'd be washed down the drain! ¹²I jumped up and down and waved my arms.

D ¹³Dad turned on the tap. ¹⁴Water poured on my head. ¹⁵It knocked me down. ¹⁶I held on to the edge of the drain as the water pulled at my legs. ¹⁷Yuck! ¹⁸A gob of toothpaste landed on my head. ¹⁹I had to escape. ²⁰I tried to climb on the toothbrush when Dad rinsed it. ²¹The water from the faucet knocked me back into the sink.

E ²²Now what? ²³Dad was closing the drain. ²⁴The sink started to fill with water. ²⁵I was treading water to stay afloat. ²⁶There was nothing for me to hold on to.

F ²⁷Dad dipped a washcloth in the water, and I grabbed it. ²⁸When he lifted the cloth to his face, I leaped on his head. ²⁹I climbed down to his ear and yelled as loud as I could. ³⁰Dad must have thought I was a fly buzzing in his ear. ³¹He shook his head and batted at his ear, knocking me off. ³²I was heading for the floor. ³³It was a long way down.

G ³⁴"Don't step on me!" I yelled.

H ³⁵"Neal, wake up," said Mom. ³⁶"It sounded like you were having a bad dream."

I ³⁷I opened my eyes and saw Mom standing over my bed.

J ³⁸"Whew!" I gasped. ³⁹"Was that scary!"

DIRECTIONS: Circle the letter next to the correct answer or write the answer on the lines given. When asked, write the number of the sentence or the letter of the paragraph that is the best evidence.

1. Where does Neal's dream take place?

   _____

   Which 2 paragraphs are the best evidence? ____, ____

2. What caused Dad to shake his head and bat at his ear?

   _____

   _____

   Which 2 sentences are the best evidence? ____, ____

3. Why do you think Dad couldn't hear Neal in sentence 7?

   _____

   _____

4. Which word best describes Neal's feelings in the dream?

   A. scared
   B. shy
   C. confident
   D. unfriendly

5. How did Neal get out of the sink?

   A. He climbed onto Dad's toothbrush.
   B. He grabbed the washcloth as Dad lifted it.
   C. He floated to the top of the sink.
   D. Dad saw him in the sink and picked him up.

   Which paragraph is the best evidence? ____

6. How do you think Mom knew that Neal was having a bad dream?

   _____

   _____

   Which sentence is the best evidence? ____

44. All About Ants by Carrie Beckwith

A [1]Ants are very social insects. [2]They live and work together to help make things run smoothly.

B [3]Most ants live in nests. [4]Ant nests are not always under sand hills. [5]Some nests are made out of leaves. [6]And some ants don't stay in one nest. [7]These ants are nomads. [8]They move from one nest to the next.

C [9]In an ant colony, every ant has a job. [10]Older ants hunt for food. [11]Younger ants have "baby-sitters" who take care of them. [12]Some ants work on building the nest. [13]Big ants guard the colony from attack.

D [14]Ants also have a leader. [15]The leader is called the queen ant. [16]She starts the ant colony by finding a place to nest. [17]Once the nest is built, she lays her eggs in it. [18]When the eggs hatch, she cares for all the baby ants. [19]Once the baby ants are grown, they become her workers. [20]They take over all of the jobs of
the nest. [21]Now the queen ant has only to lay more eggs.

E [22]The social ways of ants have helped them to become one of the most successful insects of all.

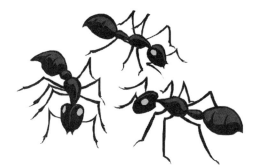

DIRECTIONS: Circle the letter next to the correct answer or write the answer on the lines given. When asked, write the number of the sentence or the letter of the paragraph that is the best evidence.

1. In sentence 7, what does the word *nomads* probably mean?

   _____

   _____

   Which 2 other sentences give context clues? ____, ____

2. What happens once the baby ants become adults? They:
   A. find a new nest.
   B. lay more eggs.
   C. take turns being the leader.
   D. take jobs in the colony.

   Which sentence is the best evidence? ____

3. What do you think might happen if ants quit working together? Give two examples.

   1. _____

      _____

   2. _____

      _____

   Which sentence is the best evidence for each example?
   ____, ____

4. What is the main idea of the story?
   A. Worker ants do most of the work.
   B. Ants have many types of nests.
   C. Ants are social insects.
   D. Ants are smart insects.

   Which sentence is the best evidence? ____

5. List the three main jobs of the queen ant.

   1. _____

      _____

   2. _____

      _____

   3. _____

      _____

   Which sentence is the best evidence for each job? ____, ____, ____

6. From reading the passage, you could say that ants are
   A. hard working.
   B. lazy.
   C. strong.
   D. not helpful.

   Which 2 paragraphs are the best evidence? ____, ____

45. A Skateboarder Speaks Out by Carrie Beckwith

July 4, 2014

Dear Editor,

A ¹Last month, I was riding my board down the city beach trail. ²I was enjoying the sunny day and the cool ocean breeze. ³The trail was crowded with people. ⁴I kept my speed down, so I wouldn't run into anybody. ⁵I wasn't out to turn anyone into a speed bump! ⁶In fact, some bikers were passing *me* by. ⁷So, I was surprised when I was stopped by the police.

B ⁸"Is there something wrong?" I asked the officer.

C ⁹"Yes," he replied. ¹⁰"You're not allowed to skateboard on the trail. ¹¹I'm going to have to give you a ticket." ¹²*What?* I thought to myself. ¹³*You can ride a bike on the trail.* ¹⁴*You can rollerblade on the trail.* ¹⁵*Your dog is allowed on the trail.* ¹⁶*But riding a board is a crime?* ¹⁷*This is unfair!*

D ¹⁸I was being careful. ¹⁹I was riding my board slowly. ²⁰I had my helmet on. ²¹Why, then, was I in trouble? ²²I see rollerblade crashes every day. ²³Most of those people don't even know how to use their brakes! ²⁴On the other hand, most boarders know a lot about their board and how to control it.

E ²⁵I think the city should rethink the law against riding a board on the beach trail. ²⁶I'm a member of this community. ²⁷I should have the right to enjoy it like everyone else.

Sincerely,

Cam Bell

DIRECTIONS: Circle the letter next to the correct answer or write the answer on the lines given. When asked, write the number of the sentence or the letter of the paragraph that is the best evidence.

1. Where did the action of the story take place?

   _____

   _____

   Which sentence is the best evidence? ____

2. What caused Cam to keep her speed down on the trail?

   _____

   _____

   Which sentence is the best evidence? ____

3. Why was Cam surprised when the police officer stopped her?
   A. She was keeping her speed down.
   B. She had already been stopped earlier.
   C. She didn't see the policeman coming.
   D. She had been passed by people on rollerblades.

   Which sentence is the best evidence? ____

4. Number the following events in the order they actually happened.

   ____ Cam writes the letter.

   ____ Bikers pass Cam on the trail.

   ____ Cam decides to ride her board on the trail.

   ____ The policeman stops Cam.

5. Using paragraphs C and D, give two reasons why Cam feels skateboarding should be allowed on the city beach trail.

   1. _____

      _____

   2. _____

      _____

   Which sentence is the best evidence for each reason?____, ____

6. What is the main idea of the letter?
   A. Cam thinks everyone should ride skateboards.
   B. Cam tells her story to gain support for her opinion.
   C. Cam thinks rollerblading should be against the law.
   D. Cam explains the problem she had on the city trail.

46. A Mystery in Time by Margaret Hockett

A ¹The year was 3020, and strange objects were appearing on our space station. ²A sword, a rug. ³Even a squealing pig. ⁴The computer said they were from ancient Earth.

B ⁵"Maybe Varga can solve the mystery," I said. ⁶She was our keeper of keys. ⁷"But Varga is missing," Toro reminded me. ⁸"Maybe she found a new job. ⁹She always did want more control."

C ¹⁰An article called "People of Ancient Earth" was found in Varga's room. ¹¹It said Earthlings were simple. ¹²They would bow to anyone with power.

D ¹³Meanwhile, the station was becoming crowded. ¹⁴"There are too many things," I decided. ¹⁵"Let's zap them to the storeroom." ¹⁶The zapper could move things instantly, so Toro went to find one. ¹⁷He came back saying, "A zapper is missing!"

E ¹⁸Something else was strange. ¹⁹The time machine was set to the year 1232 on Earth.

F ²⁰"I've figured it out!" I said. ²¹I dressed for the year 1232 and climbed into the time machine. ²²I pushed a button. ²³My seat trembled. ²⁴Soon, it was shaking hard. ²⁵Now I was in a bumpy wagon heading for a castle.

G ²⁶I sneaked through the shadows to the throne room. ²⁷People were offering gifts. ²⁸When an old man insisted he had no gifts, all became quiet.

H ²⁹The woman on the throne rose. ³⁰It was Varga! ³¹"No gifts?" she growled. ³²"I can get rid of you just like that." ³³She zapped his cane and he fell over. ³⁴People gasped in surprise.

I ³⁵I called the station and told them what to do next. ³⁶When Varga herself disappeared, the people were even more amazed than before!

J ³⁷No one saw me in the corner as I, too, quietly left. ³⁸They were staring at the things showing up in Varga's place at the throne. ³⁹A sword, a rug, a pig, and more.

DIRECTIONS: Circle the letter next to the correct answer or write the answer on the lines given. When asked, write the number of the sentence or the letter of the paragraph that is the best evidence.

1. Paragraph B mentions a mystery. What is the mystery?

   _____

   _____

2. You could say that Varga is:
   A. caring.
   B. selfish.
   C. gentle.
   D. frightened.

   Which paragraph is the best evidence? _____

3. Sentence 20 shows the narrator has figured out the mystery. Which was probably NOT a clue to the solution?
   A. information found in Varga's room
   B. the fact that a zapper was missing
   C. his dressing for the year 1232
   D. the setting on the time machine

4. The story takes place in two different settings. Give one of them.

   _____

5. Match each cause with its effect. Fill in each blank with the letter of the correct cause. (Causes are lettered A–D, results are listed below them.)
   A. The wagon ride is bumpy.
   B. The station zaps her.
   C. Varga zaps the cane.
   D. The man brings no gifts.

   _____ Varga zaps the cane.

   _____ The seat shakes hard.

   _____ The man falls down.

   _____ Varga disappears from the throne.

6. Predict what the narrator might find back at the station.

   _____

   _____

7. There was conflict between:
   A. Varga and the old man.
   B. the people on the station.
   C. the narrator and the old man.
   D. the narrator and the time machine.

   Which paragraph is the best evidence? _____

47. Island Patriot by Margaret Hockett

A   [1]It's 1838. [2]I'm in the Thousand Islands of the St. Lawrence River. [3]The islands are in a maze of waterways. [4]They make a good hiding place between Canada and the United States.

B   [5]I raise my spyglass for a look. [6]Well, if my name ain't Bill Johnston! [7]That's a British steamship headed this way. [8]Those British folks have too much power over us Canadians. [9]We need to show them who's boss, and that ship looks like an easy target.

C   [10]Not all Canadians agree with us Patriots. [11]We tried to take over Toronto's city hall last year. [12]Only 400 joined us, and we were beaten. [13]Most Patriots gave up after that. [14]But not me and my men! [15]Last May, we burned the British steamship *Sir Robert Peel*. [16]We stole the money they were going to use to pay their soldiers. [17]That really made the British mad!

D   [18]Some people call me crazy. [19]They say the British are here to stay. [20]I'll show them. [21]I'll hide in the Thousand Islands. [22]They'll search each of the paths that make up the maze. [23]But they'll get lost before they ever find me! [24]I'll make trouble until the British leave and give us freedom.

E   [25]Aha! [26]The ship is coming closer. [27]I'd better signal to my front men. [28]It's time to attack!

DIRECTIONS: Circle the letter next to the correct answer or write the answer on the lines given. When asked, write the number of the sentence or the letter of the paragraph that is the best evidence.

1. Number the events from paragraphs B and C in the order they *really* happened. The first one has been done for you.

____ Most Patriots give up.

____ Johnston sees a ship with his spyglass.

____ Johnston attacks the *Sir Robert Peel.*

_1_ Patriots are beaten in Toronto.

2. As used in sentences 3 and 22, the word *maze* probably means:
   A. system of pathways where it's easy to get lost.
   B. open waters where you can move quickly.
   C. border of three countries.
   D. amazing area for sightseeing.

   Which other sentence from paragraph D gives the best context clue? ____

3. Johnston attacked British ships because he wanted to:
   A. find more money.
   B. get back at Canadians.
   C. get attention.
   D. make the British leave.

   Which sentence is the best evidence? ____

4. The setting of the story is:
   A. a river between Canada and the U.S.
   B. islands between the U.S. and Britain.
   C. the Canadian bushlands.
   D. the British Isles.

   Which 2 sentences from paragraph A are the best evidence? ____, ____

5. Which is NOT true of the Thousand Islands?
   A. It is in the St. Lawrence River.
   B. It lies between Canada and the U.S.
   C. It could be called a maze of waterways.
   D. It contains the city of Toronto.

6. In what year did the Patriots try to take over the city hall in Toronto? _____

   Which 2 sentences are the best evidence? ____, ____

7. Mark each of the following as T for True or F for False.

   ____ All Canadians were upset by British rule.
   ____ Canadians fighting against British rule were called Patriots.

   Which sentence is the best evidence for both statements? ____

48. Meteors by Carrie Beckwith

A   ¹Shooting stars aren't really stars. ²They are pieces of rock and metal that have fallen down from space. ³Scientists call them "meteors." ⁴Most meteors are as small as a grain of dust. ⁵Some are bigger than a school bus!

B   ⁶Meteors dash across the sky every day. ⁷On a clear night, away from bright city lights, you may see up to five in one hour. ⁸Their white trails are best seen when it is pitch black. ⁹Meteors fall from space at very high speeds, creating lots of heat. ¹⁰The high speed and heat cause most meteors to burn up before they hit the ground. ¹¹However, some meteors *do* hit Earth.

C   ¹²Sometimes meteors come down like rain. ¹³When this happens, we call it a "meteor shower." ¹⁴During a shower, you can see about 100 meteors an hour! ¹⁵Meteor showers happen when dust from a comet falls down to Earth.

D   ¹⁶Look up at the night sky. ¹⁷See if you can find any meteors. ¹⁸Maybe you'll be the lucky one who sees a shower of them.

DIRECTIONS: Circle the letter next to the correct answer or write the answer on the lines given. When asked, write the number of the sentence or the letter of the paragraph that is the best evidence.

1. What is the main idea of paragraph A?
   A. Scientists call meteors shooting stars.
   B. Meteors can be bigger than a school bus or as small as dust.
   C. Shooting stars are not meteors.
   D. Meteors are pieces of rock and metal that fall into our sky.

2. Would city lights make it harder for you to see meteors? Use paragraph B to explain your answer.

   _____

   _____

   _____

   _____

   Which sentence is the best evidence? ____

3. What causes most meteors to burn up?
   A. high speed and heat
   B. the passing of a comet
   C. dust and heat from the sun
   D. the fall from space

   Which sentence is the best evidence? ____

4. In paragraph C, what can result from a passing comet?

   _____

   _____

   Which sentence is the best evidence? ____

5. The story suggests that meteors are different sizes.

   Which 2 sentences are the best evidence? ____, ____

49. A Long Distance Adventure by David White

A ¹One summer morning, Kyoko tried to call her cousin in New York. ²For a moment, nothing happened. ³Then, she saw a flash of light and found herself standing outside the Empire State Building! ⁴She had been sitting on the living room couch. ⁵Now she was in New York City.

B ⁶The streets and sidewalks were crowded and very noisy. ⁷She tried to ask for help but couldn't make herself heard over the din.

C ⁸A cat darted into the busy traffic. ⁹A boy ran after the cat. ¹⁰"Look out!" Kyoko yelled, as she jumped out and grabbed the boy's hand. ¹¹She dragged him back onto the sidewalk as a big truck sped by. ¹²The cat made it to the other side. ¹³The boy would not have been so lucky.

D ¹⁴The boy turned out to be the son of the mayor of New York City. ¹⁵"I can't thank you enough," the mayor told Kyoko. ¹⁶"Scott had run down the street and left his mother behind." ¹⁷The mayor and Kyoko posed for a picture together. ¹⁸He promised she could have anything. ¹⁹She asked for a phone so she could call home. ²⁰She dialed her parents' number. ²¹Nothing happened at first. ²²One flash of light later, she was back on the living room couch.

E ²³Her parents didn't know she had been gone most of the day. ²⁴They arrived home from work that evening. ²⁵She didn't tell them about her day. ²⁶They thought she made up too many stories anyway. ²⁷Besides, the phone trick wasn't working anymore. ²⁸She had called her friend Lisa but hadn't left the house. ²⁹Her father wanted to know if she had noticed anything wrong with the TV at home. ³⁰"My radio wouldn't work for three full hours," he said. ³¹"It must have been something in the air. ³²Other people noticed it, too."

F ³³The next day, Kyoko's father was reading the newspaper. ³⁴"Look at this," he said. ³⁵"Here's a photo from New York of a girl who saved the mayor's son's life."

G ³⁶"She looks just like Kyoko!" her mother gasped. ³⁷"Her parents must be so proud of her."

H ³⁸Kyoko smiled a secret smile.

DIRECTIONS: Circle the letter next to the correct answer or write the answer on the lines given. When asked, write the number of the sentence or the letter of the paragraph that is the best evidence.

1. What is the most likely meaning of *din*, as used in sentence 7?

   A. telephone ringing
   B. loud noise
   C. tall buildings
   D. long distance

   Which other sentence gives the best context clue? ____

2. Kyoko's actions in paragraph C can best be described as:

   A. tricky.
   B. brave.
   C. selfish.
   D. mistaken.

3. What made Kyoko disappear?

   A. dialing the phone
   B. talking to Lisa
   C. chasing a cat
   D. meeting the mayor

   Which 2 sentences from paragraph D are the best evidence? ____, ____

4a. Why did Kyoko grab the boy's hand and drag him back onto the sidewalk?

   _____

   _____

   _____

4b. Circle the group of sentences that best supports your answer.

   1–4   5–9   10–13

5. What would Kyoko's parents probably say if she told them the girl in the photo was her?

   _____

   Which sentence from paragraph E is the best evidence? ____

6. Which of the following are the two places where the action takes place?

   A. Kyoko's house and Lisa's house
   B. Lisa's house and New York City
   C. New York City and Kyoko's house
   D. Kyoko's house and the mayor's house

   Which 2 sentences are the best evidence? ____, ____

7. What is the main idea of paragraph C?

   A. A cat darts out into traffic.
   B. A boy runs after the cat.
   C. Kyoko grabs the boy's hand.
   D. Kyoko rescues the boy.

50. Masai Culture by Carrie Beckwith

A   ¹The Masai tribe live in the grasslands of East Africa. ²Their way of living centers around their cows.

B   ³Caring for the cows takes a lot of time. ⁴Women and girls milk the cows every morning. ⁵The men and boys watch over the cows during the day. ⁶They must protect them from attack. ⁷They must also keep them healthy. ⁸At night, the cows are kept inside the village. ⁹The village is surrounded by a fence made of thorn bushes. ¹⁰The thorn fence protects the cattle and the tribe from being eaten by lions. ¹¹When the cows have eaten all the grass, the Masai migrate to new land. ¹²The whole village leaves in search of fresh grassland.

C   ¹³The Masai live in huts called "bomas." ¹⁴The women of the tribe make bomas from sticks, grass, and cow droppings, or dung. ¹⁵The dung is patted onto a dome-shaped frame of sticks and grass. ¹⁶When the dung dries, it hardens and becomes strong. ¹⁷But during heavy rains, the women may patch the boma every day.

D   ¹⁸The blood of a cow is used in special celebrations. ¹⁹When a boy is old enough to become a warrior, there is a big feast. ²⁰The Masai use an arrow to cut a vein in the cow's throat. ²¹A small amount of blood is taken. ²²The blood is then mixed with milk and drunk during the meal. ²³It is a special treat for the Masai.

E   ²⁴The Masai have been living this way for over a thousand years. ²⁵They are highly respected because they are one of the last tribes in Africa that have held onto their old ways.

DIRECTIONS: Circle the letter next to the correct answer or write the answer on the lines given. When asked, write the number of the sentence or the letter of the paragraph that is the best evidence.

1. What is the main idea of the article?
    A. The Masai spend a lot of time caring for their cows.
    B. The Masai's way of living centers around their cows.
    C. The warrior celebration is very important.
    D. The Masai are respected because they have held onto their old ways.

    Which sentence is the best evidence? ____

2. What causes the Masai to move to new land?

    _____

    _____

    _____

    Which sentence is the best evidence? ____

3. What is done with the cow's blood when a boy becomes a warrior?

    _____

    _____

    _____

    Which sentence is the best evidence? ____

4. Which sentences in paragraph B support the main idea that caring for cows takes a lot of time.
    A. 4, 5
    B. 9, 10
    C. 14, 17
    D. 3, 4

51. *Seven Kisses in a Row*
   by Patricia MacLachlan (Excerpt)

A   [1]"I am not going to sleep in my bedroom tonight," announced Emma.

B   [2]"Why not?" asked Zachary. [3]"Because of the mess?"

C   [4]"No," said Emma. [5]"Because of night rumbles."

D   [6]"What are night rumbles?" asked Zachary.

E   [7]"I am not sure," said Emma, "but my friend Noah has them. [8]He says they only come at night. [9]He says they will come here soon. [10]They are furry things with legs who live in the closet, and whiskery shadows in the corners of the room, and a long arm that lives under the bed and tries to grab you when you jump into bed."

F   [11]"Have you seen them yet?" asked Zachary.

G   [12]Emma shook her head. [13]"Not yet. [14]And I am not going to."

H   [15]"Where will you sleep?" asked Zachary.

I   [16]"In the backyard," said Emma. [17]"In the tent."

J   [18]"In the tent!" exclaimed Zachary. [19]He loved sleeping in the tent. [20]"But what about bugs and grubs and wild wolves?"

K   [21]"I am not afraid of bugs and grubs," said Emma. [22]"And Wayne will protect me from wild wolves. [23]In the tent there are not a lot of corners with boxes and closets and chairs and toy chests for things to hide in. [24]Or in back of. [25]Or under."

L   [26]"No mess," said Zachary, nodding.

M   [27]"No mess," agreed Emma. [28]She began to pack her things.

DIRECTIONS: Circle the letter next to the correct answer or write the answer on the lines given. When asked, write the number of the sentence or the letter of the paragraph that is the best evidence.

1. Who is the main character in the story?

   A. Wayne
   B. Zachary
   C. Emma
   D. Noah

2. The story suggests that Emma's room is:

   A. tidy.
   B. messy.
   C. empty.
   D. bright.

   Which 3 sentences are the best evidence? ____, ____, ____

3. Why is Emma going to sleep in the tent?

   A. She wants to get away from the night rumbles.
   B. She loves sleeping in the tent.
   C. She is afraid of the bugs and grubs.
   D. She is camping with her friend Noah.

   Which sentence is the best evidence? ____

4. Write the number of the sentence that describes the night rumbles.

   Sentence ____

5. Which of the following does Emma conclude?

   A. The tent has bugs.
   B. The tent is more fun.
   C. The tent is safer.
   D. The tent is in the back yard.

   Which sentence is the best evidence? ____

52. *Chocolate Fever*
by Robert Kimmel Smith (Excerpt)

A   ¹"I'm Dr. Fargo," said the doctor, "that much I know. ²Now what I'd like to do is get to know more about those brown spots of yours." ³He wet the tip of a cotton swab and brushed it gently against one of the big brown spots on Henry's arm.

B   ⁴"Ouch," said Henry.

C   ⁵"Did that hurt?"

D   ⁶"No."

E   ⁷"Then why did you say 'ouch'?"

F   ⁸"Because," said Henry, "I *thought* it was going to hurt."

G   ⁹"I see," said Dr. Fargo. ¹⁰Shaking his head, he put the cotton swab into a glass jar. ¹¹"Take this to the laboratory at once," he said to one of his assistants, and the man rushed out of the room.

H   ¹²"In a few minutes we'll know more about those big brown spots of yours," the doctor said. ¹³Hands behind his back, he began to pace the room. ¹⁴Suddenly he stopped, his nose in the air. ¹⁵"Who has been eating a candy bar in my office?" he demanded.

I   ¹⁶No one answered.

J   ¹⁷Dr. Fargo's nose twitched from side to side as he sniffed the air. ¹⁸"I smell candy," he said. ¹⁹"Someone's been eating a candy bar."

K   ²⁰Just then the telephone rang, and Dr. Fargo bounded across the room to answer it. ²¹"What—what?" he said into the phone. ²²"Are you sure?" ²³His white mustache bounced up and down as Dr. Fargo sank slowly into a chair. ²⁴He put the telephone down, a look of amazement on his face. ²⁵"Chocolate," he said. ²⁶"Those big brown spots . . . are pure chocolate . . . ."

L   ²⁷"Chocolate?" gasped Nurse Farthing.

M   ²⁸"Chocolate?" exclaimed Henry Green.

N   ²⁹"Chocolate?" echoed Dr. Fargo's two assistants.

O   ³⁰"Exactly," said Dr. Fargo. ³¹"The boy, it seems, is nothing more than a walking candy bar!"

DIRECTIONS: Circle the letter next to the correct answer or write the answer on the lines given. When asked, write the number of the sentence or the letter of the paragraph that is the best evidence.

1. Why did Dr. Fargo swab the brown spot?

   _____

   _____

   Which paragraph is the best evidence? ____

2. What caused Henry to say "Ouch"?

   _____

   _____

   Which sentence is the best evidence? ____

3. Which of the following actions supports the idea that Dr. Fargo was eager to learn the results?

   A. He sent the swab to the lab right away.
   B. He smelled a candy bar.
   C. He put the swab in a glass jar.
   D. His nose twitched as he smelled the air.

   Which sentence is the best evidence? ____

4. What was Dr. Fargo really smelling when he smelled a candy bar?

   _____

   _____

   Which sentence is the best evidence? ____

5. Which of the following words means almost the same as *bounded* in sentence 20?

   A. grabbed
   B. tied
   C. leaped
   D. walked

6. What is the main idea of the story?

   A. Henry smells like a candy bar.
   B. Dr. Fargo finds out Henry's spots are chocolate.
   C. The assistants are surprised at the test results.
   D. Dr. Fargo tests Henry's spots.

POSTTEST: **Grandfather's Medal** by Cheryl Block

A   [1]"Ramon, please give me that," demanded Mrs. Ortiz sharply. [2]Ramon had brought the medal to show his friend Juan. [3]It was his grandfather's medal from the war.

B   [4]"I'll put it away," he promised.

C   [5]"I'm sorry, Ramon, but you know the rules." [6]Sadly he handed the medal to Mrs. Ortiz. [7]How could he have been so careless? [8]He shouldn't even have the medal.

D   [9]At lunch, he went up to Mrs. Ortiz's desk to get it. [10]"I'm sorry, Ramon, but I don't want you to be distracted again. [11]I'll keep it in my desk until after school."

E   [12]He started to beg, but he knew it was useless. [13]She stuck to the rules, especially the one about paying attention in class.

F   [14]School was almost over when a messenger came for Mrs. Ortiz. [15]"Excuse me, class. [16]I must leave. [17]Miss Finch will stay with you." [18]She was gone before Ramon could say anything. [19]When the bell rang, everyone raced out. [20]Ramon waited for Mrs. Ortiz. [21]Finally, he went to the office.

G   [22]Mrs. Ortiz had left for the day! [23]Ramon couldn't believe it. [24]The medal was still in her desk. [25]He had to get it back. [26]If his father found the medal missing, he might never forgive Ramon.

H   [27]Ramon raced back to the classroom. [28]The door was still open. [29]No one was around. [30]He went to the desk. [31]The drawer was locked! [32]He couldn't find the keys. [33]He didn't know what to do. [34]He couldn't let his father down. [35]He'd promised never to touch the medal.

I   [36]He looked in the closet for a tool to open the drawer. [37]There was a hammer on the shelf. [38]Ramon got the drawer open just as the janitor came in the door.

J   [39]"What are you doing?" he yelled. [40]Ramon froze as the drawer spilled out on the floor.

DIRECTIONS: Circle the letter next to the correct answer or write the answer on the lines given. When asked, write the number of the sentence or the letter of the paragraph that is the best evidence.

1. Why did Ramon take the medal from home?

   _____

   _____

   Which sentence is the best evidence? _____

2. Which of the following class rules does Ramon break?
   A. Wait your turn to talk.
   B. Pay attention in class.
   C. Be polite to others.
   D. Be on time.

   Which paragraph is the best evidence? _____

3. What is Ramon's conflict in paragraphs G and H?

   _____

   _____

   _____

4. How does Ramon solve his conflict?

   _____

   _____

   Which paragraph is the best evidence? _____

5. Which of the following is the best moral for the story?
   A. Family is more important than friends.
   B. It is okay to take something if it really belongs to you.
   C. It is important to pay attention in school.
   D. It is important to think before you act.

6. Which two actions below support the idea that Ramon doesn't think things through?
   A. He broke into the teacher's desk drawer.
   B. He showed the medal to Juan.
   C. He handed the medal to Mrs. Ortiz.
   D. He took his grandfather's medal.

7. Which words below mean almost the same as *be distracted* in sentence 10?

   A. follow the rules
   B. go to sleep
   C. get ready
   D. not pay attention

   Which other sentence gives the best context clue? _____

8. How do you predict Ramon's father will react?

   _____

   _____

   Which 2 sentences are the best evidence? _____, _____

POSTTEST: Track and Field by Cheryl Block

A [1]Track and field is a sport that has events in running, jumping, and throwing. [2]In most events, an athlete competes against other single athletes.

B [3]Running races include the sprint, the marathon, and the relay. [4]In the sprint, a runner must be the fastest in a short distance. [5]The marathon is a long-distance race. [6]Not only must a runner be fast, he or she must also have endurance in order to finish the full twenty-six miles. [7]The relay, unlike most of the running events, has teams of runners who race. [8]Each team has four runners. [9]Each runner runs only part of the race. [10]Team members pass a stick called a baton to the next runner. [11]The last runner must race to the finish line carrying the baton in order to win the race for his team.

C [12]The high jump, the long jump, and the triple jump are three of the jumping events. [13]A high jumper must leap over a bar without knocking it down. [14]The highest jump wins. [15]The long jumper goes for length. [16]A triple jumper also goes for length. [17]A triple jumper, however, must do three different jumps in a row. [18]He must hop, step, and then leap.

D [19]Throwing events include the discus throw and the javelin toss. [20]The discus is a flat, round object thrown while the thrower stands inside a small circle. [21]The thrower tosses it as far as possible. [22]If he steps outside the circle, his throw does not count. [23]The javelin looks like a hunting spear. [24]It is thrown from a runway. [25]The athlete takes a running start before he throws the javelin as far as he can.

E [26]Track and field is a sport that offers athletes many different challenges.

DIRECTIONS: Circle the letter next to the correct answer or write the answer on the lines given. When asked, write the number of the sentence or the letter of the paragraph that is the best evidence.

1. Which of the running races requires speed and endurance?

_____

Which sentence is the best evidence? _____

2a. Which of the following words could replace the word *endurance* in sentence 6?

A. speed
B. ability to last
C. ability to jump
D. height

2b. Which part of sentence 6 gives the best context clue?

_____

_____

3. What might happen if a runner misses the baton?

_____

_____

Which sentence is the best evidence? _____

4. In sentence 7, why is the relay race unlike most events?

_____

_____

Which sentence from paragraph A is the best evidence? _____

5. What is the main idea of the article?

A. Track and field is a sport that includes many different events.
B. Track and field includes several running events.
C. The discus throw and the javelin toss are two track and field events.
D. Jumping includes the high jump, the long jump, and the triple jump.

6. The javelin is tossed from a runway because:

   A. it is thrown from a running start.
   B. it is thrown a short distance.
   C. it must be thrown from a circle.
   D. it is used for hunting.

   Which sentence is the best evidence? ____

7. What does paragraph B suggest about the last runner in a relay race?

   A. He runs the whole race.
   B. He passes the baton many times.
   C. He races against his own team.
   D. He never passes the baton.

   Which sentence is the best evidence? ____

ANSWER KEY

The answer key provides the following information: questions with the reading skill in parentheses, the correct answer given in bolded text, the numbers or letters of the evidence sentences or paragraphs, an explanation of the answer (when necessary), and reading levels are given for each story.

Although we give a recommended answer choice for each question, teachers should discuss any different responses with students to clarify their reasoning. If the teacher feels a student has made a valid case for a response, based on the evidence in the passage, the teacher may want to accept the student's answer, also.

For the short answer questions, students do not have to follow the suggested wording exactly as long as they include the key information needed to answer the question. The literature and fiction stories, in particular, are open to greater interpretation than the nonfiction as to author meaning. The primary focus of this program is to get students to think about what they read and to improve their understanding of the material. You may find your students involved in a lively debate as to which is the best answer to a question. By all means, encourage this!

PRETEST

Mighty Hunter (p. 2)
Reading Level: 2.7

1. In sentence 3, what does the word *freeze* mean? (vocabulary)
   A. become hard
   B. stay still
   C. become cold
   D. pop out
   Best context clue: **4**

   "Stares" in sentence 4 suggests that the eyes keep looking at (stay still on) some object.

2. According to paragraph A, what causes the kitten to jump when he sees something move? (cause/effect)
   his instinct
   Best evidence sentence: **5**

   A cat's hunting instinct will cause him to react when he sees something move.

3. In paragraphs A and B, the action takes place: (setting)
   A. inside, in the kitchen.
   B. outside, in the jungle.
   C. inside, in the living room.
   D. outside, in the woods.
   Best evidence sentence: **9**

4. Kittens use their hunting skills when: (inference)
   A. playing.
   B. eating.
   C. sleeping.
   D. crying.
   Best evidence paragraph: **C**

   Sentence 11 suggests that it is movement that causes him to chase and use other hunting skills.

5. Skitter is a 1-year-old cat. She lives indoors and is fed by her owners. Now she is outdoors and is hungry. She sees a mouse moving in the grass. Predict what she will do. (prediction)
   A. nothing
   B. chase it
   C. make friends with it
   D. run away from it
   2 best evidence paragraphs: **C, D**

   Paragraphs C and D suggest that a cat will develop hunting skills and use them as needed—even if it is raised indoors and fed by humans.

6. In paragraph D, what four things help a cat to hunt? (supporting detail)

eyes, ears, balance, muscles

3 best evidence sentences: **24, 25, 26**

7. The main idea of the story is that kittens' play is really: (main idea)
   A. something they learn.
   B. foolishness.
   C. hunting practice.
   D. just for fun.

Bandit (p. 6)
Reading Level: 3.8

1. Where did the last part of the story take place? (setting)

   The last part of the story took place outside, by the garbage cans.

   2 best evidence sentences from paragraph G: **19, 20** or **19, 22**

2. Why did Peter decide to look through the trash for his homework? (cause/effect)

   He thought Krista had thrown away his homework.

   Best evidence sentence: **16**
   (Also acceptable: **18**)

3. What do you think Krista saw inside the hole that Bandit dug? (inference)
   A. her homework and an old blanket
   B. Peter's homework and an old bone
   C. her doll and Peter's homework
   D. bits and pieces of Bandit's old bone

   3 best evidence sentences: **27, 28, 29**

   The pink ruffle was probably from the dress of the doll that Krista was missing, and the crumpled bits of paper with Peter's name on it were probably pieces of his homework.

4. Which of the following shows the conflict in the story? (plot)
   A. Peter is upset with the dog.
   B. Krista and Peter argue over Peter's missing homework.
   C. Mom doesn't believe that Peter finished his homework.
   D. Krista thinks Peter is stealing stuff.

   2 best evidence sentences: **16, 17**

5. Which of the following words means almost the same as *convinced* in sentence 18? (vocabulary)
   A. wrong
   B. sure
   C. pretending
   D. lucky

   Peter is sure that he is right, which is why he goes to the trouble of digging through the trash. A, C, and D do not make sense in the context of the story.

6. You can tell from the story that Peter sometimes: (character traits)
   A. gets As and Bs in his classes.
   B. jumps to conclusions.
   C. hides things from Krista.
   D. takes Bandit for walks.

   2 best evidence paragraphs: **F, G**

   Before Peter has determined what has happened to his homework, he jumps to the conclusion that his sister must have thrown it away.

7. What do you think Peter will do if he learns that his homework is missing again? (prediction)
   A. He will blame his sister Krista.
   B. He will check Krista's doll bed in her bedroom.
   C. He will go through the trash cans.
   D. He will look for covered holes in the back yard.

   Bandit is the culprit in the story, so Peter will probably check outside to see if he may have buried his homework again. A and C are not likely, since

Peter will have discovered by the end of the story that it was not his sister who took his homework. It was Bandit. B does not make sense.

8. Peter did not believe his sister when she told him that she did not throw away his homework. (supporting detail)

   2 best evidence sentences: **18, 20**

INFERENCE

1. Wagons West (p. 14)
Reading Level: 4.0

1. The child was to fill the bucket with water.

   True

   Evidence: **3, 5**

   The river has water in it.

2. The sun was still shining brightly.

   False

   Evidence: **4**

3. The child didn't move when he first saw the bear.

   True

   Evidence: **7**

4. In sentence 5, the rustle was made by the bear.

   True

   Evidence other than 5: **6**

5. The bear was thirsty.

   True

   Evidence: **10**

6. The bear was hungry.

   No evidence

7. The bear was surprised by the bucket.

   True

   Evidence: **13**

8. The bear chased the child.

   No evidence

2. Why Dogs Wag Their Tails (p. 16)
Reading Level: 2.8

1. Why did the dog tell the cat, "You're no help"?

   The cat told the dog to purr. The dog probably could not purr.

   Best evidence sentence: **4**

2. Why did the hyena suggest that the dog should laugh?
   A. He wanted to make fun of the dog.
   B. Laughing made the hyena happy.
   C. Purring made the dog sound silly.
   D. He was worried about the dog.

   Best evidence sentence: **9**

3. What did the chimp think would happen if the dog smiled? The dog would:
   A. look happy.
   B. say he was sorry.
   C. stop looking for friends.
   D. become the chimp's friend.

   Best evidence sentence: **16**

4. In sentence 22, why did the lion tell the dog to think of something happy?

   The lion wanted to see how the dog would show his happiness.

   Best evidence sentence: **27**

5. What does the last paragraph suggest about how the dog felt when he left the lion?

   He was happy.

   His wagging tail meant that the dog was happy.

   Best evidence sentence: **35**

3. Did Time Stand Still? (p. 18)
Reading Level: 3.2

1. In sentence 13, what time did the narrator probably think it was?
   A. 9:00
   B. 12:00
   C. 8:00
   D. 10:00
   Best evidence sentence from paragraph B: **8**

   (Sentence 9 is acceptable, provided the student justifies that answer by pointing out that without 9, the reader does not know she believed the captain.)

2. In sentence 16, she probably changed her watch to what time?
   9:00

   Best evidence sentence: **14**

3. What if you flew from California to Ohio? For each time zone, you should: set your watch
   A. one hour earlier.
   B. one hour later.
   C. two hours later.
   D. where it already is.

   Best evidence sentence from paragraph E: **24**

   The story describes traveling from Ohio to California and each zone from east to west is one hour earlier. California to Ohio is the opposite direction, so zones are one hour later.

4. In sentence 17, why was she hungry?
   It was 1:00 p.m. in Ohio, where she started. 1:00 p.m. was her lunchtime.

   Best evidence sentence from paragraph D: **19**

5. Altogether, the narrator was in how many time zones? (diagram)
   four

The map shows four zones from Ohio to California. The story says she was flying to California and she started from Ohio.

4. An Old-fashioned Saturday (p. 20)
Reading Level: 3.1

1. The sled is powered by:
   A. motor
   B. pedals
   C. animal
   D. the sun
   2 best evidence sentences from paragraph A: **1, 2**

   A whinny is a noise made by a horse.

2. When does the story action take place?
   A. weekend
   B. holiday
   C. school day
   D. not known
   See the story title. Saturday falls on the weekend.

3. What does the narrator mean by "what can Ma say?" in sentence 8?
   A. He wonders what she could say.
   B. She can't complain that he's wet.
   C. She wants him to come home.
   D. He thinks she wants him soaked.
   The narrator is contrasting the statement with the fact that he gets soaked. He suggests that she can't complain because she's the one who wanted him to go out in the first place (9).

4. What kind of liquid is in the bucket?
   sap

   Best evidence sentence from paragraph C: **13**

   In sentence 13, pouring "without spilling any sap" suggests that the bucket contains sap.

5. What kind of syrup will they have after the sap is boiled?
   A. apple
   B. corn
   C. pine
   D. maple

   Best evidence sentence: **12**

   We can tell from sentence 12 that they are gathering *maple* sap, so it must turn into maple syrup.

6. Read sentence 16. What must happen before the sled goes to the sugar shack?
   A. All buckets must be gathered.
   B. Sap must be gathered until the tank is filled.
   C. One more bucket must be poured.
   D. The sled must be pulled to the sugar shack.

   The narrator has been gathering and pouring buckets of sap into the tank. Sentence 16 implies that the tank must be full before going to the sugar shack. Therefore, sap must be gathered until the tank is filled.

5. **Teeger** (p. 22)
   Reading Level: 3.5

1. What was Teeger?
   A. a housecat
   B. a classmate
   C. a zoo animal
   D. a toy tiger

   1 best evidence sentence: **5**

2. How did Cari think Teeger felt while she was gone?
   She thought he was lonely.

   (Also acceptable: **bored***)

   1 best evidence paragraph: **A**
   (Paragraph E would support bored*.)

3. Who most likely put the glasses on Teeger?
   A. Mom
   B. Cari
   C. Teeger
   D. no one

   Best evidence sentence from paragraph E: **20**

   Paragraph E suggests that Cari is happy that Teeger is enjoying himself. Sentence 20 suggests that Mom is the one who helped him "enjoy" himself.

4. How did it make Cari feel to think that Teeger was doing new things around the house?
   A. sad
   B. happy
   C. angry
   D. lonely

   Best evidence paragraph: **E**

5. Which sentence in paragraph D suggests that Cari uses her imagination?
   17

   Sentence 17 suggests that after Cari saw Teeger at the piano, she imagined she had heard his music.

6. At the end of the story, Cari thanked her mother. She probably did this because she thought her mother:
   A. fed Teeger his meals.
   B. helped Teeger enjoy himself.
   C. didn't let Teeger outside.
   D. kept Teeger from getting dirty.

   Just before she thanked her mother in sentence 20, sentence 19 suggested that Cari thought Teeger was enjoying himself. (She probably decided her mother was the one who put Teeger in the places where he could enjoy himself.)

6. **Lead On, Sacagawea** (p. 24)
Reading Level: 4.5

1. Sacagawea spoke two Native American languages. Why did Lewis and Clark think this would help?

She could help them talk to the natives.

2 best evidence sentences: **9, 10**

2. Which of these might be another reason Lewis and Clark hired Sacagawea to lead them west?
A. **She could get them fresh food.**
B. She could carry extra supplies for them.
C. She knew how to paddle a boat.
D. She knew how to use native plants.

Best evidence sentence: **13**

3. Why did the explorers probably NOT cross the mountains in winter?

Since the mountains were snowy even in spring, they were probably too snowy in the winter.

Best evidence sentence: **19**

4. Which of these probably best explains why the explorers traveled by boat in some places?
A. They were more comfortable in boats than on horses.
B. The boats had more room for supplies than the horses did.
C. The rivers went directly to the west coast.
D. **It was usually faster than traveling on land.**

Best evidence sentence: **20**

5. What does sentence 3 suggest about travelers who would go west after Lewis and Clark?
A. They would go in pairs.
B. **They would go there to stay.**
C. They would follow the same route.

D. They would take Native American guides.

7. **The Barn** (Excerpt) (p. 26)
Reading Level: 3.4

1. In sentence 9, what does Nettie think is foolish?

Ben trying to talk with father

Best evidence paragraph: **B**

2. How does Ben probably feel in paragraph F?
A. happy
B. strong
C. **unsure**
D. mad

Best evidence sentence: **15**

Ben wonders if he is mistaken, which shows that he is feeling unsure.

3. Why do you think Ben asked Father to close his eyes in paragraph K and then move them again in paragraph N?
A. He wasn't sure if Father heard him the first time.
B. **He wanted them to believe Father understood them.**
C. He was proud that his father could do it.
D. He didn't see Father blink the first time.

Ben keeps trying to convince Nettie and Harrison that Father is capable of communicating. Having Father do two different things shows them Father does understand. There is no evidence for A or D. C may be true, but it is not the main reason Ben asks Father to move his eyes again.

4. Why do you think Nettie said, "Oh, mercy...," in sentence 31?
A. She still didn't believe that her father could understand them.
B. She was frightened by Ben's shouting.

C. **She believed that Father could hear them.**

D. She was tired of playing foolish games with Father.

Nettie said "Oh, mercy" after Father responded a second time to Ben's request that he close his eyes.

5. Why does Ben clap his hands with glee in the last sentence of the story?

He has proven that Father can understand them.

8. *Sable* (Excerpt) (p. 28)
Reading Level: 4.1

1. Sable is not only a good watchdog, she is also:
A. a smart dog.
B. a good runner.
C. **a good hunter.**
D. a small dog.
Best evidence sentence: **1**

2. How is Tate feeling in sentences 5 and 7?
A. uncaring
B. **worried**
C. sorry
D. pleased

3. Which two sentences support the idea that Doc will give Sable a good home?
Sentences **11, 22**

4. Based on the story, which of the following is true about Doc?
A. **He used to have a dog.**
B. He used to have a cat.
C. He doesn't like animals.
D. He likes to hunt rabbits.
Best evidence sentence: **12, 13**

5. Where do you think Doc probably lives?
A. **in the country**
B. in an apartment
C. at the beach
D. on an island
Best evidence sentence: **25**

Sentence 25 tells us that Doc owns land. Sentence 23 supports sentence 25, suggesting that Doc has lots of land. There is no evidence for the other choices.

VOCABULARY

9. **Frontier Women** (p. 34)
Reading Level: 2.7

1. Which of the following words means almost the same as *settle* in sentences 1 and 10?
A. enjoy
B. **stay on**
C. pay for
D. discover
Best context clue from paragraph A: **2**

B is the best choice. Sentence 2 says that they wanted to make new homes there. Paragraph C also describes the hard work they had to do to settle the land, so A doesn't make sense. There is no evidence for C or D.

2. What does the word *journey* mean in sentence 5?

trip

Best context clue from paragraph A: **4**

Sentence 4 uses *trip* as a synonym for the word *journey*. This is supported by sentence 1, which says they were moving west.

3. In sentence 11, what is meant by "the land had to be cleared"?

They had to chop down trees and remove rocks.

Best context clue: **12**

4a. In paragraph E, how do you know that the word *chores* means jobs?

The paragraph tells about the different jobs that girls did.

4b. Write an example of a chore from paragraph E.

Accept any of the following examples: **fix meal, clean house, look after children, plant crops, care for animals**

10. Lizard On the Loose (p. 36)
Reading Level: 3.8

1. Which part of sentence 6 help you figure out that *cautiously* means carefully?

to make sure the lizard didn't jump out

2. Which word below can be used instead of *jostled* in sentence 9?
   A. held
   B. bumped
   C. liked
   D. missed

Best context clue: **8**

B is supported by sentence 8; the kids were pushing. Ernie was jostled accidentally, so A doesn't work. Neither C nor D make sense in the context because neither would cause him to hit the box.

3. Paragraph C says some of the kids *pursued* the lizard. What did these kids do to the lizard?

They chased it.

Since the lizard got away, it makes sense that they would chase it in order to catch it. This is reinforced by sentence 15, which says they couldn't catch it. Sentence 17 repeats that they were continuing to pursue, or chase, the lizard.

4. What do you think a *commotion* is in sentence 20?
   A. classroom
   B. party
   C. bell
   D. noise

D is the best choice since we know a commotion is something Mr. Purdy heard. Choice A is incorrect because, in this context, classroom means the room, and you couldn't substitute *classroom* for *commotion*. We know the class wasn't having a party, so B is incorrect. There is no evidence for C.

5. Which of the following is the best meaning for the word *elated* in sentence 26?
   A. worried
   B. sorry
   C. joyful
   D. quiet

C is the best choice. Mei was worried when the lizard got loose. Now he is safe, so A is incorrect. Neither B nor D makes sense in this context.

11. George Washington Comes to Class (p. 38)
Reading Level: 3.7

1. Sentence 1 uses the words *droning on*. Choose the words that come closest to the meaning of *droning on*.
   A. speaking in a dull voice
   B. speaking with love
   C. speaking excitedly
   D. speaking as if singing

Best context clue: **2**

Sentence 2 uses the word *boring* to describe the teacher's story. Boring is a synonym for dull. Sentence 3 also helps because it tells us the student is getting sleepy because of the teacher's droning. Therefore, choice A makes the most sense.

2a. As used in sentence 4, what does the word *descending* mean?

falling, dropping, or going down

Words like *falling* make sense. In sentence 4, his eyelids are compared to the tree; both are falling.

2b. Which part of sentence 3 gives you a clue to the meaning of *descending*?

starting to fall

3. In sentence 9, the word *pierce* means *go through*. What part of sentence 9 gives you a clue to the meaning of *pierce*?

like arrows

The word *pierce* means to cut or go through, so the words *like arrows* support the meaning.

4. Which part of sentence 19 gives you a clue to the meaning of *survey*?

measure borders

12. **Desert Survivor** (p. 40)
Reading Level: 3.8

1. The word *shallow* most likely means:
A. near the surface.
B. deep underground.
C. full of water.
D. spread out.

A is supported by sentences 8 and 9. Sentence 8 gives us a choice between A and D. However, sentence 9 clarifies that shallow roots must be near the surface in order to take in rain. Sentence 7 tells us that other roots are shallow rather than deep, so B is incorrect. C does not make sense when substituted in both sentences.

2. Which part of sentence 9 helps you understand what *shallow* means?
A. can take in water
B. from even a light rain
C. are not deep
D. these shallow roots

3. Write the part of sentence 8 that helps you understand what *shallow* means.

stay near the surface

4. Which of the following means almost the same as *absorbs* in sentence 12?
A. throws away
B. squeezes
C. takes in
D. replaces

C is the best choice because the phrase *through its outer skin* supports the idea that the stem takes in water. This is also supported by sentence 11, which compares the stem to a sponge. A sponge *takes in* liquid and holds it. Choice A is the reverse of this, so it is incorrect. There is no evidence for B or D.

5. Write the part of sentence 14 that helps explain the meaning of the word *expand* in sentence 13.

get bigger

This answer is also supported if you substitute the words *get bigger* for *expand* in sentence 13.

13. **New World for the Old** (p. 42)
Reading Level: 4.1

1. What is the meaning of the word *elderly*, as used in sentence 5?
A. aged
B. human
C. sad
D. unwanted
Best evidence sentence: **1**

The old people in sentence 1 are the missing elderly in sentence 5. The word *aged* is another synonym for old. None of the other choices are supported.

2. The word *glimpsed* in sentence 8 means to have a quick look. Write the part of sentence 9 that supports this meaning.

looked again

Her first look, or glimpse, was too quick. She didn't see enough, so she looked again.

3a. In sentence 12, the word *investigating* means:
A. seeing.
B. running away from.
C. pushing.
D. checking out.

3b. Which two sentences together give you the best evidence?
A. 14, 15
B. 15, 16
C. 11, 12
D. 13, 14

Together, sentences 11 and 12 give the meaning of investigating. *Checking out* is mentioned just before the word is used. Also, the narrator *felt* something while investigating, suggesting that *feeling* (a form of checking out) is related to *investigation*.

4. Sentence 19 uses the word *assortment*. If you had an *assortment* of toys, they would probably all:
A. be the same.
B. have movable parts.
C. look new and unusual.
D. be different.

Part of sentence 19: **no two things were alike**

5. If you *assumed* something, as in paragraph L, you would probably:
A. think it was true.
B. think it was wrong.
C. grow old.
D. disappear.

Choice A is supported by "they knew they would go" in sentence 35. B, C, and D make no sense in the context.

6. A *resident* (sentence 39) is probably:
A. someone who lives in a place.
B. someone who gets lost easily.
C. one of many robots.
D. one of many whirligigs.

Since the resident will fill a bed, A

makes sense. There is no evidence for B, C, or D.

14. **Help Solve the Garbage Problem**
(p. 44)
Reading Level: 4.3

1. Write the three words from sentence 15 that best show the meaning of the word *recycle*.

using it again

2. The word *reduce* in sentence 6 means:
A. add to.
B. bury.
C. lessen.
D. burn.

Best evidence sentence from paragraph A: **5**

C is the best answer because sentence 5 states that we have *too much* garbage. If we want to correct the problem, as stated in sentence 6, then we would want to lessen, or *reduce*, garbage.

3a. Read the definition of *organic* in sentence 21. Which of the following is NOT made of organic materials?
A. wooden comb
B. plastic cup
C. watermelon
D. pea soup

A plastic cup is made from manmade materials.

3b. Circle the items below that *are* organic.
coffee grounds
color photo
pine needles
banana peels
nail polish

Coffee grounds, pine needles, and banana peels come from plants. Color photos and nail polish contain manmade agents.

4. Using sentence 27, you can tell that the word *decay* means:
   A. start growing.
   B. break down.
   C. stay the same.
   D. turn into flowers.

B is the best answer because sentence 27 states that as the materials decay, they break down. There is no evidence to support A or D. C is contradicted by the fact that organic materials become part of the soil, thus they do change.

STORY PARTS

15. A View From Above (p. 52)
Reading Level: 2.5

1. From where is the narator telling the story? (setting)
   in a balloon

   Best evidence sentence: **1**

2. Summarize the plot. (plot)
   The narrator goes for a balloon ride, sees lots of things, hears insects and birds, then lands.

3. What is the conflict described in paragraph E? (conflict)
   The narrator has to land but doesn't want to end his ride.

   Best evidence sentence: **26**

4. Put the following events in the order in which they happened in the story. (sequence)
   2 Narrator sees island (11)
   5 Balloon touches down (28)
   3 Sun begins to set (21 or 22)
   1 Balloon flies straight (5)
   4 Narrator takes pictures (23)

5. What do we learn about the narrator from the story? (character)
   A. He likes to watch birds.
   B. He enjoys nature.
   C. He is a painter.
   D. He is afraid of heights.

   B is supported by his description of his balloon ride. There is no evidence for the other choices.

6. What time of year is it in the story? (setting)
   A. spring
   B. summer
   C. fall
   D. winter

   Best sentence each from paragraphs B and C: **9, 18**

16. A Foolish Wish (p. 54)
Reading Level: 3.0

1. Where does the story take place? (setting)
   On a road on the way to market. (or town)

   2 best evidence sentences: **1, 2**

2. Where is the well located? (setting)
   A. just outside town
   B. on a hill
   C. near his house
   D. in the middle of town

   Best evidence sentence: **9**

   A is the best choice because the boy stops at the edge of town, which is just outside the town. There is no evidence for B, C, or D.

3. Which of the following is a main event in the story? (plot)
   A. He was thrilled.
   B. He found a coin.
   C. He was going to market.
   D. He walked back home.

   Finding the coin started the events that led up to the climax, throwing the coin in the well. The other choices are details within the story.

4. Why was the boy foolish? (character trait)

He threw away his coin because he believed the story.

2 best evidence paragraphs: **D, E**

Sentence 20 tells us he realized he was foolish. As a result of his actions in paragraphs D and E, he lost his coin, his wish, and the chance to sell his eggs. Sentence 10 tells us that *some* people believed this was a wishing well, but there was no real evidence that this was true.

5. How did the boy probably feel at the end?
A. cheerful
B. disappointed
C. uncaring
D. frightened

2 best evidence sentences: **20, 21**

6. Summarize the results of the boy's actions. (summary)

The boy lost his gold coin, didn't get his wish, and didn't get to sell his eggs.

Best evidence paragraph: **E**

17. First Wave (p. 56)
Reading Level: 3.2

1. Number the events of the story in correct time order. (sequence events)
1 Jonah puts on his wetsuit. (1)
3 Jonah turns his board around. (23)
2 Dad spots a wave. (17)
4 Jonah gets his feet on the board. (35)

2. In paragraph A, you can tell that Jonah is: (character)
A. nervous.
B. silly.
C. angry.
D. bored.

2 best evidence sentences: **7, 8**

Sentences 7 and 8 explain that Jonah's heart was beating fast, so he was probably excited and nervous. Sentence 7 also tells us his heart didn't quite believe he'd be fine.

3. What made Jonah scream "Yes!" in sentence 36? (character)

He was finally riding a wave. (Also acceptable: **He was excited that he finally made it up on the board.**)

Best 2 evidence sentences: **35, 38**

4. Use paragraphs A and B to describe both the time and place of the story. (setting)

It is morning. The story moves from the beach to the ocean.

Best evidence sentence in paragraph A: **3**

Best evidence sentence in paragraph B: **9** (Also acceptable: **12**)

5. What is Dad trying to do with Jonah? (plot)

He's trying to teach him how to surf.

18. Surprise Vacation (p. 58)
Reading Level: 3.4

1. Number the following events in the story in the correct time order. (sequence)
1 Dad tells the family that they're going to Hawaii. (4)
3 Sean trips over his bag on his way back to the kitchen. (17)
4 Dad points to the date on the calendar. (20)
2 The kids pack their bags. (12)

2. Describe where most of the story takes place. (setting)
in the kitchen

2 best evidence sentences: **2, 16**

3. During what part of the day does the story take place? (setting)

morning

Best evidence sentence: **2**

4. You can guess from Dad's actions that he: (character)
   A. is hard working.
   B. **likes to joke.**
   C. is very serious.
   D. likes to travel.

   2 best evidence paragraphs: **A, F**

5. In paragraph B, how can you tell that the kids were happy about going to Hawaii? Give two examples. (character)

   1. They sang. 2. They ran to their rooms to pack.

   2 best evidence sentences: **8, 12** (Also acceptable: **7, 12**)

6. What did their big brother do after Dad pointed to the date? (sequence)

   (Accept one or both of these ideas.) **He lifted his head and started laughing.**

   2 best evidence sentences: **21, 22**

19. A Puff of Smoke (p. 60)
Reading Level: 3.4

1. How did the parents first react to Dino? (character)
   A. They were very angry.
   B. They were frightened.
   C. **They were surprised.**
   D. They weren't interested.

   Best evidence sentence: **8**

2. In what room did the boy put the egg? (setting)

   in his bedroom

   Best evidence sentence: **3**

   A dresser is usually found in the bedroom.

3. What is the most important event in paragraph B? (plot)
   A. A squeaking sound wakes up the boy.
   B. The boy names the dragon Dino.
   C. **A dragon hatches from the egg.**
   D. The boy shows the dragon to his parents.

   The dragon hatching from the egg caused further events to happen in the story. The other three choices are supporting details related to this main event.

4. When did Dad move Dino to the back yard? (sequence)
   A. when he outgrew the box
   B. after he hatched
   C. **when he started knocking things over**
   D. after he set Mr. Mickles' tree on fire

   Best evidence sentence: **18**

5. According to paragraph F, how would you describe Dino? (character)
   A. **gentle**
   B. fierce
   C. shy
   D. silly

   2 best evidence sentences: **27, 28**

   A is supported by the fact that Dino let the kids ride on him and that he roasted marshmallows for them. They weren't afraid of him, so this rules out B. He liked to be with the kids, so this rules out C. There is no evidence to support D.

20. Invisible Spy (p. 62)
Reading Level: 4.7

1. Which of the following is a key event in the story? (plot)
   A. Maisy is in the newspaper.
   B. Maisy steps on a twig.
   C. Maisy is paid by the government.
   D. **Maisy puts her invention to use.**

   Best 2 evidence paragraphs: **E, F**

2a. Maisy could be described as a
_____ kind of girl. (character)
A. wimpy
B. crazy
C. take-charge
D. do-nothing

2b. Of the following sentences, which best
supports your answer?
A. 5
B. 14
C. 20
D. 24

Maisy had to do a lot of work and make
decisions herself to record the men and
go to the police, so C is correct. A, B,
and D are not supported.

3. Describe the setting of the main action
in the story.

**The action takes place outdoors in
a park.**

Best evidence paragraph: **F**

4. Number the following events in the
order they happened in the story.
1 Mr. Pikes is threatened. (3, 4)
4 Bad guys go to jail. (21)
2 Maisy steps on a twig. (16)
3 Maisy goes to the cops. (20)

5. The main conflict in the story is
between Maisy and whom or what?

**The main conflict is between Maisy
and the bad guys** (or the actions of the
bad guys).

21. *Dexter* (Excerpt)   (p. 64)
Reading Level: 2.4

1. Where does the story take place?
(setting)
A. out in the open field
B. in the deepest timber
C. on the banks of a creek
D. by the seashore

Sentences 2 and 3 tell us they are on
the bank of a creek. Sentences 5 and
30 support this idea, so C is the best
answer. B is contradicted by sentence 1.
There is no evidence for A or D.

2a. The main conflict is between: (conflict)
A. Dave and himself.
B. Dexter and Dave.
C. Dexter and Mr. Ogle.
D. Dave and Mr. Ogle.

2b. Explain the conflict.

**Dave doesn't want Mr. Ogle to
shoot the pony, and Mr. Ogle
doesn't want Dave telling him what
to do.**

2 best evidence paragraphs. **F, G**

3. Paragraph K shows that Mr. Ogle also
has a conflict with himself. Describe the
conflict. (conflict)

**He wants to shoot but can't with
Dave and the pony looking at him.**

4. What can you tell about Mr. Ogle from
the passage? (character)
A. He lets nothing get in his way.
B. He doesn't believe in killing.
C. He is affected by others.
D. He is a patient hunter.

Best evidence sentence: **24**

Paragraphs I and K show that Mr. Ogle
can't shoot the pony while the boy and
the pony are watching him.

5. What goal seems most important to
Dave? (character)
A. saving the pony
B. telling Mr. Ogle what to do
C. driving the horses
D. keeping people from hunting

Paragraphs A, D, and F suggest that
Dave's purpose is to keep Mr. Ogle from
shooting Dexter, the pony.

6. Number the events in the order they happened. (sequence/plot)

2 Mr. Ogle tells Dave to go away. (17–18)

1 Dave yells to stop Mr. Ogle. (6, 9–10)

4 Dave's eyes are blurred. (29)

3 Mr. Ogle puts the rifle over his shoulder. (25)

MAIN IDEA

22. Your Sense of Taste (p. 70)
Reading Level: 3.0

1. What is the main idea of the story?
   A. Your tongue gives you your sense of taste.
   B. The tip of your tongue tastes sweet things, like ice cream.
   C. The taste buds on your tongue never stop working.
   D. Your nose and tongue create your sense of taste.

   2 best evidence sentences: **2, 3**

2. What is the main idea of paragraph B?
   A. Your taste buds sense sweet and salty tastes.
   B. Pizza tastes sweet and salty.
   C. Ice cream has lots of sugar in it.
   D. Your tongue uses its taste buds to sense flavors.

   Best evidence sentence: **4**

3. Paragraph B supports the main idea of the story by telling about:
   A. your nose and how it works to create your sense of taste.
   B. your tongue and how it works to create your sense of taste.
   C. how ice cream and pizza taste.
   D. taste buds and how they work.

4. What is the main idea of paragraph C?
   Your nose affects your sense of taste. (Also acceptable: **Your sense of smell affects your sense of taste.**)

   Topic sentence: **12**

5. Which sentence number below best supports the main idea of paragraph C?
   A. 15
   B. 16
   C. 14
   D. 13

23. The Wright Stuff (p. 72)
Reading Level: 4.1

1. What is the main idea of the story? (main idea)
   The Wright brothers invented the airplane.

2. Which of these sentences is the main idea of paragraph B? (main idea)
   A. Sentence 4
   B. Sentence 5
   C. Sentence 6
   D. Sentence 7

3. Which of the following sentences would most likely fit in paragraph E? (supporting detail)
   A. Airplanes can carry just a few people or more than a hundred.
   B. The gliders also tipped over in the air.
   C. They started in 1900 and kept at it.
   D. Wilbur even went to France to show off the new invention.

   D is correct because it is an example of what the Wright Brothers did to make their invention famous, which is the main idea of paragraph E. A has nothing to do with the story. B fits in paragraph C, not E. C is incorrect because paragraph E is all about what happened after the first flight in 1903.

4. Which of these sentences is NOT a supporting detail of paragraph E? (supporting detail)
   A. Sentence 14
   B. Sentence 15
   C. Sentence 16
   D. Sentence 17

   A is correct because it is the topic sentence, or main idea, of the paragraph. B, C, and D are supporting details.

5. Which of these sentences from paragraph F best supports the whole story? (supporting detail)
   A. They fly around the world.
   B. They fly high in the air.
   C. The Wright brothers' ideas live on.
   D. They fly at night.

   C is correct because it talks about the Wright brothers' ideas, which grew into the invention of the airplane. A, B, and D are supporting details.

24. **False Face Society** (p. 74)
   Reading Level: 4.5

1. What is the main idea of the story? (main idea)
   A. The False Face Society performed with masks to cure the sick.
   B. The False Face Society carved many types of masks.
   C. The masks had healing powers and were needed to keep away evil spirits.
   D. The False Face Society knew how to cure many sicknesses using ashes from a fire.

2. No one knew who the members of the False Face Society were. Which two sentences are the best evidence? (supporting detail)

   5, 6

3. What is the main idea of paragraph B? The False Face Society: (main idea)
   A. wore masks to hide their faces.
   B. danced with rattles.
   C. made noises to scare away the evil spirits.
   D. tried to cure people's sickness.

   Sentence 5 states that the False Face Society was believed to cure sickness. So, D is the correct answer because paragraph B describes *how* they tried to cure sickness. A, B, and C are details of what they would do to cure sickness.

4. What would a member do with the ashes from the fire? (reading for detail)

   He would rub it on the sick person's head.

   Best evidence sentence: **11**

5. What is the main idea of paragraph D? (main idea)

   There were many types of masks, but some parts of the mask were always the same.

   Best evidence sentence: **18**

   Everything that follows sentence 18 expands upon the main idea.

6. In paragraph D, which three things on the mask were always the same? (supporting detail)

   They all had big noses, strange mouths, and horse hair.

   2 best evidence sentences: **19, 22**

THEME —————————————

25. A Nutty Modern Folktale (p. 78)
Reading Level: 3.6

1. What is the theme of the story?
   A. An accident brings people together.
   B. People can invent great things in times of trouble.
   C. People have different ideas about how to live.
   D. A wall is the best way to separate people.

   Best evidence paragraph: **A**

   A is the best choice for theme because the new sandwich created when the factory crumbled brought the Jammers and Nutters together. B and C are details within the story. There is no evidence for D.

2. Which of these sentences from paragraph B gives the main idea of the paragraph?
   A. The Nutters ate only peanut butter on bread.
   B. The Jammers ate only jam on bread.
   C. The two groups were not at all alike.
   D. They even ate different foods.

   C is the main idea. A, B, and D are details that support the main idea.

3. Look at the following sets of sentences from paragraph B. Which set best supports the idea that the two groups of people liked different types of food?
   A. 3 and 4
   B. 5 and 6
   C. 7 and 8
   D. 9 and 10

   D tells what the two peoples ate on their sandwiches. A and B do not talk about food. C is not as specific.

4. What is the main idea of paragraph C? The wall:
   A. kept both sides together.
   B. was high enough that nobody could climb over.
   C. kept both sides separate.
   D. was built on both sides of the factory.

5. How does the rest of paragraph D support the main idea—that the factory fell down?
   It tells what happened to the factory after the earthquake.

26. Home Away From Earth (p. 80)
Reading Level: 3.8

1. Which sentence is the topic sentence of paragraph B? (topic sentence)
   Sentence 6

   In this case, the topic sentence is the second sentence in the paragraph. Most of the paragraph describes how Mars was strange.

2. What is the main idea of paragraph D? (main idea)
   A. Shigai's favorite color is green.
   B. No green plants grow on Mars.
   C. Shigai misses the green plants from home.
   D. There are only rocks and sand on Mars.

   Sentences 15 and 18 support B as the main idea. C and D are supporting details. There is no evidence for A.

3. Which of the following is the best theme for this story? (theme)
   A. Humans can't win against Nature.
   B. There is no place like home.
   C. People must adjust to a new place.
   D. Mars is an unusual planet.

   C is the best choice because most of the story describes the difficulties of settling on Mars. There is no evidence for A. B is mentioned at the beginning of the story, but the idea does not run throughout the story. D is a supporting detail of the story. The theme is based on the characters' struggle to live on Mars.

4. Which sentence from paragraph A best supports the idea that Shigai is tired of living on the ship? (supporting detail)
   Sentence 3

   Sentence 4 tells us specifically that Shigai wanted a home again. Sentence 3 gives reasons why he felt that way.

5. Which sentence from paragraph F best supports the idea that dust storms were dangerous? (supporting detail)
   Best evidence sentence: **25** (Also acceptable: **26**)

6. Why was the colony being built underground? (reading for detail)
   to protect them from the planet's surface

   Best evidence sentence: **11**

27. Giant Hoax (p. 82)
   Reading Level: 4.5

1. Paragraph B tells *mainly* about: (main idea)
   A. how Doakers built their houses.
   B. problems caused by the giants.
   C. Doakers discovering the giants.
   D. how the Doakers lived their lives.

2. What is the theme of the story? (theme)
   A. Jokers get what they deserve.
   B. Only giants play tricks.
   C. Life is unfair to little people.
   D. It's hard to stop once you start playing tricks.
   Best evidence paragraph: **F**

   The giants played jokes on the Doakers. As a result, the Doakers got back at them in a way that drove the giants crazy.

3. Use paragraph D to list three things the Doakers did to get back at the giants. (supporting details)
   1. They removed the insides of some fruit. 2. They tied a giant's beard in knots. 3. They glued a giant's fingers together.

4. In paragraph F, which of the following drove the giants crazy? (supporting details)
   A. They were sorry for their tricks.
   B. They ran away from Doaker land.
   C. Their beards and fingers were stuck together.
   D. They couldn't see any tiny people.

   2 best evidence sentences in paragraph F: **26, 27**

5. In two or three sentences, give a summary of the story. (summary)
   The giants played tricks on the Doakers. The Doakers found out about the giants and their trickery. They played tricks back on the giants, finally causing the giants to leave.

28. *The Cricket in Times Square* (p. 84)
Reading Level: 5.0

1. What is the main idea of paragraph A? (main idea)
   A. **Chester worries that Tucker won't escape the cat.**
   B. The fights between cats and mice in Connecticut are one-sided.
   C. Tucker Mouse is going to be killed.
   D. Tucker Mouse is Chester's new friend.

   Throughout paragraph A, Chester is fretting over Tucker's supposed enemy, the cat. B is a detail. There is no real evidence for C or D.

2. Which paragraph best supports the idea that cats and mice in Connecticut do not get along? (supporting details)

   Best evidence paragraph: **A**

3. Which sentence best shows Harry Cat being friendly? (supporting detail)

   19

4. What did Chester do to try to warn Tucker about the cat? (reading for detail)

   He made signs so that Tucker would look up and see the cat.

   Best evidence sentence: **10**

5. What could be the theme of this passage? (theme)
   A. When things get tough, don't give up.
   B. Friends make life more interesting.
   C. **Things are not always what they appear to be.**
   D. The city is no place for a cricket.

   C is the best answer because Chester thought all cats and mice were enemies. He learned, however, that Harry Cat and Tucker Mouse are best friends and that in New York cats and mice don't fight.

CAUSE/EFFECT

29. **High-Rise Doghouse** (p. 90)
Reading Level: 2.6

1. In paragraph C, what will cause you to build a new house?
   The old house will be too crowded.

   Best evidence sentence: **7**

2a. What results every time more dogs come to live in the doghouse?
   A. Dogs share windows.
   B. The roof is replaced.
   C. The house becomes wider.
   D. **The house height doubles.**

   Each illustrated stage shows a height that is double that of the stage before. Sentence 14 states that you will need a house that is twice as tall. There is no evidence for A, B, or C.

2b. How do the pictures help you to prove your answer?
   The houses go from 2 feet tall to 4 feet tall to 8 feet tall. Also, each house has twice as many windows as the one before.

3. By the end of paragraph D, we can tell there will be six dogs. How do we know?
   Paragraph B tells us there are three dogs. Paragraph D says each dog will find another. There will be twice as many dogs, so there will be six.

4. What will cause you to make a high-rise doghouse?
   each dog asking a relative to move in

   Best evidence paragraph: **F**

5. Too many dogs have too much fun in a too tall house. Which of the following will probably NOT be a result?
   A. You will build again.
   B. The house will sway.
   C. The dogs will be afraid.
   D. The dogs will run away.

   Best evidence paragraph: **G**

   Choice A is contradicted by sentences 25–27. Therefore, it is indeed NOT a result. B, C, and D are all mentioned in paragraph G.

30. Cat and Mouse (p. 92)
Reading Level: 2.8

1. In sentence 3, why didn't the cat go through the hole?
   He couldn't fit.

   Signal word in sentence 3:

   Since

2. What caused the cat to jump back in sentence 7?
   The boxes came tumbling down.

   1 other evidence sentence: **6**

3. Why was the cat rubbing his nose in sentence 13?
   A. His nose itched.
   B. The mouse ran away.
   C. The jar hit him.
   D. The board hit him.

   Best evidence sentence: **12**

4. What was the result when the cat tipped over the trash can?
   A. The trash can was dented.
   B. The cat jumped into the can.
   C. The cat got hurt.
   D. The cat was covered with trash.

   Best evidence sentence: **19**

31. Streetball Hero (p. 94)
Reading Level: 3.5

1. Why were the street lights flickering?
   They were flickering because it was getting dark.

   (Also acceptable: **They were flickering because they were starting to come on.**)

   Signal word: **since**

2. Why did Ty stay outside even though his mom was calling for him?
   He wanted to finish up the game. (Also acceptable: **It was the last inning of a close game.**)

   3 best evidence sentences: **3, 4, 5**

3. Ty was a little nervous because:
   A. he didn't want to skid on the street.
   B. his mom was calling for him.
   C. the pitcher was really good.
   D. the crowd was growing loud.

   Best evidence sentence: **8**

4. What caused Ty to swing and miss?
   A. the noise
   B. Ameko's pitch
   C. the darkness
   D. his nerves

   Best evidence sentence: **19**

5. What happened as a result of Ty skidding across the street?
   He won the game for his team.

   Best evidence sentence: **33**

6. What caused Ameko to miss the ball?
   The darkness. She was looking into the night sky.

   Best evidence sentence: **26**

32. Northern Lights (p. 96)
Reading Level: 3.8

1. Paragraph A suggests that you feel small because:
   A. the bands are so big.
   B. the fingers are huge.
   C. the searchlights move.
   D. you are looking upward.
   Best evidence sentence: **7**

2. The sights in paragraph A are a result of:
   A. a fireworks display.
   B. a laser show.
   C. a natural show.
   D. searchlights.
   Best evidence sentence: **12**

3. The Northern Lights are NOT a result of:
   A. the sun's storms.
   B. Earth's being like a magnet.
   C. bands waving in the air.
   D. bits from the sun.
   Best evidence paragraph: **C**

4. Why does the air near the North Pole trap the fragments from the sun?
   A. The air is thick.
   B. Earth is like a magnet.
   C. The air is clean.
   D. The pole is close to the sun.
   Best evidence sentence: **18**

5. In each sentence below, underline the cause and circle the effect.
   1. When these fragments come through the air, they cause the air to glow.
   2. The air conditions make the light move in different patterns.

6. According to paragraph E, what happens when the Northern Lights are seen?
   They create joy for many people.
   Best evidence sentence: **26**

33. Space Chase (p. 98)
Reading Level: 3.7

1. What caused the loud noise Jade and Vi heard?
   A space jet caused the noise.
   Best evidence sentence: **3**

2. Why was it hard for Vi to see the jet?
   It went by so fast.
   Best evidence sentence: **5**

3. What caused the Galaxy Cruiser pilot to panic?
   A. He saw the Galaxy Cruiser behind him.
   B. He saw the Starship start to drop.
   C. He saw the Starship flip on its side.
   D. He thought the enemy jet would hit the Starship.
   2 best evidence sentences: **12, 13**

4. What caused the enemy jet to come down?
   The stream of laser fire from the Galaxy Cruiser hit the enemy jet.
   2 best evidence sentences: **25, 26**

5. Why were the girls waiting on the landing?
   A. They were waiting for a friend to get off the ride.
   B. They wanted to ride on the jet.
   C. They wanted to get a better view of the enemy pilot.
   D. They were forced to move there.
   2 best evidence sentences: **34, 35** (Also acceptable: **7, 8**)

34. The Secret of Popcorn (p. 100)
Reading Level: 4.6

1. Put in order the events that cause a kernel to pop.
   4 The starch pops out. (12)
   3 The kernel turns inside out. (11)
   1 The heat turns the water layer to steam. (6)
   2 The pressure pushes the outer layer. (9)

2. What causes the water to turn into steam?
   A. water
   B. starch
   C. heat
   D. pressure
   Best evidence sentence: **6**

3. What two things mentioned in the story could keep a kernel from popping?
   A kernel loses 3 percent of its water. A kernel is not heated to 400°F.

   2 best evidence sentences: **14, 16**

4. What would happen if you heated popcorn kernels to 350°? The popcorn would be
   A. stuck together.
   B. white and fluffy.
   C. hard kernels.
   D. corn on the cob.
   Best evidence sentence: **16**

35. "Tracks" *From The Stories Huey Tells*
(Excerpt) (p. 102)
Reading Level: 3.7

1. Why did Huey go down to the basement?
   A. to find Julian's book
   B. to get the hammer
   C. to check the clock
   D. to find a flashlight
   Best evidence sentence: **7**

2. Why did Huey use a hammer to make the prints?

It made deeper prints.

2 best evidence sentences: **15, 16**

3. In paragraph C, how was Huey able to see as he worked?
The moon gave him light.

Best evidence sentence: **9**

4. Why was Julian excited?
He thought a zebra had been at the house.

Best evidence sentence: **21**

5. What made Huey's dad believe that these were zebra tracks?
   A. He matched them with Julian's book.
   B. He saw the zebra.
   C. He looked at them.
   D. He carefully measured them with a ruler.
   Best evidence sentence: **23**

PREDICTION ———————————

36. Missing Ring (p. 106)
Reading Level: 3.0

1. Where do you predict the ring will be found? (prediction)
   A. in a trash can
   B. in a donut hole
   C. in the food line
   D. in the kitchen
   3 best evidence sentences: **16, 24, 28**

2a. What would probably happen if Pudge tried to read the symbols in the code ring? (prediction)

He would not understand what the symbols meant.

2b. Why?

He would need the code book. Sam still has it.

Best evidence paragraph: **A**

3. What will Jose probably do next time someone hands him something important? (prediction)

He will probably make sure he holds on to it.

Best evidence sentence: **14**

4. What will Darla probably tell Sam she saw? List two things. (prediction)

(Accept any two) **1. She saw Pudge with his hands in his pockets. 2. She saw a donut peeking out of Pudge's jacket. 3. She saw Pudge glance at Sam and Jose.**

Best evidence paragraph: **F**

37. **The City Street Game** (p. 108)
Reading Level: 3.1

1. Predict what would happen if Jenny ran around the yellow fire hydrant before she ran around the red fire hydrant.
A. She would hear the word "Stop!"
B. She would have to run back to Tree 1.
C. She would say her name.
D. She would have to wait until she heard "Go."

Best evidence sentence: **18**

2. What would probably happen if Jenny heard the word "Stop" while she was passing a house?
A. She would fail the test.
B. She would stop moving.
C. She would start over.
D. She would say her name.

Best evidence sentence: **13**

3. Predict what could happen if no one yelled the word "Stop" during Jenny's game.

Jenny could run down the whole block without having to stop. (Also acceptable: **She could win the game.**)

4. Does Jenny have a good chance of passing the test? Explain your answer.

Yes. She is good at new games.

2 best evidence sentences: **20, 21**

38. **Real Pirates** (p. 110)
Reading Level: 3.2

1. Based on paragraph A, predict how the people would feel if the pirates did NOT invade the town.
A. disappointed
B. tired
C. pleased
D. satisfied

Paragraph A implies that people like it when the pirates invade. Sentence 8 says the mayor was smiling, and sentence 9 says it was a great show.

2. What would a tourist probably do if she saw someone dressed as a pirate robbing someone on the street during Pirate Days?
A. stop him
B. call the police
C. pay no attention
D. watch him

2 best evidence sentences from paragraph C: **18, 19**

3. Let's say one of the robbers from the story wanted to rob people at the circus. How would he probably dress?
A. as a gang member
B. as a clown
C. as a pirate
D. as a robber

Best evidence paragraph: **B**

Paragraph B shows that the men know enough to wear what makes them fit into the crowd.

4. What would Ruth probably do if there were no sock in her mouth?
   A. take a bow
   B. pretend to be mad
   C. say nothing
   D. yell for help

   Best evidence sentence from paragraph D: **23**

5. Based on paragraph H, predict what the girl will do next.
   A. take the sock from Ruth's mouth
   B. give up and go home
   C. untie the cops
   D. just watch the parade as it passes

   Choice A makes the most sense since Ruth seems to be the only other person who knows the truth. (People would believe Ruth because she is an adult and because they had thought she was part of the show.) Paragraph H implies that the girl will try to make them believe her, so B and D are unlikely. Paragraph G indicates that the cops don't believe her and that they are able to untie themselves, so C is unlikely.

39. Pinch, Pull, Coil (p. 112)
Reading Level: 3.5

1. In paragraph C, what might your pot look like if you didn't turn it?
   A. The sides could stay thick all around.
   B. The sides could be uneven.
   C. There would be no difference.
   D. The sides could be thin all around.

   Best evidence sentence: **9**

2. Based on the pictures, how will the shape change if you overlap the coils? (diagram)
   The sides will not be straight up and down. (Also acceptable: **It will not be a cylinder.**)

   Best evidence paragraph: **F**

3. In paragraph E, what could happen if you roll the coil from the outside ends to the center?
   It could break.

   Best evidence sentence: **16**

4. In paragraph E, what might happen if you forget to press the coils on the inside?
   A. You wouldn't have a solid wall inside.
   B. The coils would stick together.
   C. You couldn't cut the ends of the coils.
   D. You couldn't add more coils.

   Best evidence sentence: **20**

   A is the best choice based on sentence 20. The coils already stick together, so B is incorrect. You cut the coils before you press them together, so C is incorrect. There is no evidence for D.

5. What could happen if you didn't bake your pot?
   It would not get hard.

   (Also acceptable: **It would stay soft.**)

   Best evidence sentence: **26**

40. Eddy the Bully (p. 114)
Reading Level: 3.6

1. Besides Eddy and Josh, who else might get into trouble with the principal? Explain why.
   Rosy. She started the rumor that got Josh into trouble with Eddy.

   2 best evidence sentences: **1, 2**

2. What do you think will happen to Eddy if he doesn't quit fighting?
   He'll get kicked out of school again.

   Best evidence sentence: **8**

3. What do you think would have happened if Mrs. Hicks had not shown up?

There would have been a fight. (Also acceptable: **The crowd would have stayed.**)

Best evidence sentence: **30**

4. If Eddy got into a fight with someone at your school, what would he probably do before he started to fight?

He would ask the kid a few questions.

Best evidence sentence: **6**

5. Do you think Josh would fight if a smaller kid picked a fight with him? Explain your answer.

No. He might try to talk his way out of it, since he says he's a thinker and not a fighter. He also explains that he wants to protect his head.

3 best evidence sentences: **11, 12, 13**

41. How Lies Are Detected (p. 116)
Reading Level: 4.6

1. Let's say your friend earned an F but lied and said he got an A. As he lied, what would probably happen to his heart rate? It would:
   A. slow down.
   B. speed up.
   C. stay the same.
   D. disappear.

   Best evidence sentence: **6**

   Sentence 6 implies that your heart may beat faster when you lie.

2. What would happen if the pens were removed before your lie detector test?
   A. No chart would be made.
   B. You would have no heart beat.
   C. The waves would increase.
   D. You would be called a liar.

   Best evidence sentence: **12**

3. If someone gave you a lie detector test but didn't care about your hand sweat response, he might leave off:
   A. the pens.
   B. the chart.
   C. a finger clip.
   D. an arm sleeve.

   Best evidence paragraph: **B**

   Since the four devices measure your hands sweating, your heart rate, and your breathing, it is logical to assume one of the finger clips is used to measure the sweat response.

4. Rob Banks is accused of stealing money. He takes a lie detector test. Which question will he most likely be asked first?
   A. Did you steal the money?
   B. Where were you during the robbery?
   C. Is your name Rob Banks?
   D. What kind of pizza do you like?

   2 best evidence sentences: **15, 16**

   Since you are first given simple questions, and one includes your name (sentence 16), C is correct. The fact that you must answer with *yes* or *no* rules out choices B and D. The question in choice A is important to the case. (Sentence 19 implies this type of question would be given *after* the simple ones.)

5. You answer all the questions on a lie detector test. Two of your "yes" responses make wave patterns different from your normal truth pattern. What will the test reader think?

   Your answers to the two questions may have been lies.

   Best evidence paragraph: **C**

42. *Sideways Stories From Wayside School* (Excerpt)   (p. 118)
Reading Level: 2.2

1. Let's say Mrs. Jewls gives Joe nine bananas. She tells him to count like she showed him in paragraph J. How many bananas will Joe say there are?
   A. ten
   B. nine
   C. five
   D. none

   Paragraphs J and M (also P and Q) show that Joe counts from one to ten and gives an answer of ten when he tries to count the way the teacher does.

2. Let's say Joe is given seven oranges. He is asked to tell how many there are. What does he say?

   He says there are seven.

   3 best evidence paragraphs: **A, E, S**

   Joe comes up with the right number when he counts his own way (sentences 2, 11, and 35).

3. What would happen if Joe were to count correctly *and* get the right answer? Mrs. Jewls would:
   A. say he counted wrong.
   B. say he got the wrong answer.
   C. let him go to recess.
   D. keep him inside to do math.

   2 best evidence sentences from paragraphs C and D: **6, 7**

4. Let's say Mrs. Jewls shows Joe eleven marbles. What two possible answers might he give?

   He would say either ten or eleven.

   Explain your answer.

   He either counts her way and ends up with ten or he counts his way and ends up with the right answer.

5. Paragraphs C and D show how Mrs. Jewls helps Joe with counting. What would Mrs. Jewls probably do if a student had trouble with her alphabet letters? Mrs. Jewls would:
   A. not do anything.
   B. punish her later.
   C. send a book home.
   D. help her at school.

   Since Mrs. Jewls is working with Joe on his counting during recess, it is reasonable to assume she would do something similar if a student had trouble with her letters.

MIXED SKILLS

43. Down the Drain   (p. 120)
Reading Level: 2.4

1. Where does Neal's dream take place? (setting)

   bathroom

   2 best evidence paragraphs: **A, C** (Also acceptable: **A, D**)

2. What caused Dad to shake his head and bat at his ear? (cause/effect)
   When Neal yelled in his ear, Dad thought it was a fly.

   2 best evidence sentences: **29, 30**

3. Why do you think Dad couldn't hear Neal in sentence 7? (inference)
   Since Neal was so small, his voice was probably little, too.

4. What word best describes Neal's feelings in the dream? (character traits)
   A. scared
   B. shy
   C. confident
   D. unfriendly

   There are several instances where Neal was scared. Neal was afraid he'd be washed down the drain or drown in the sink. So A is the best choice. There is no evidence for B, C, or D.

5. How did Neal get out of the sink? (reading for detail)
A. He climbed onto Dad's toothbrush.
B. He grabbed the washcloth as Dad lifted it.
C. He floated to the top of the sink.
D. Dad saw him in the sink and picked him up.

Best evidence paragraph: **F**

B is correct because Neal grabbed the washcloth when Dad lifted it. Then he jumped on Dad's head. A is incorrect because the water knocked him back into the sink. D is incorrect because Dad didn't see him. There is no evidence for C.

6. How do you think Mom knew that Neal was having a bad dream? (inference)
He probably yelled out loud.

Best evidence sentence: **34** (Also acceptable: **36**)

44. All About Ants (p. 122)
Reading Level: 3.0

1. In sentence 7, what does the word *nomads* probably mean? (vocabulary)
Nomads are ants that don't stay in one nest. They move from one nest to the next.

2 other context clues: **6, 8**

2. What happens once the baby ants become adults? They: (sequence)
A. find a new nest.
B. lay more eggs.
C. take turns being the leader.
D. take jobs in the colony.

Best evidence sentence: **19**

(Also acceptable: **20**)

3. What do you think might happen if ants quit working together? Give two examples. (predict)
Accept any two. **1. They would get hungry or starve. 2. Baby ants might die if no one took care of them. 3. The nest would not get built. 4. The colony might get attacked.**

Best evidence sentence per example: **10, 11, 12, 13** (respectively)

4. What is the main idea of the story? (main idea)
A. Worker ants do most of the work.
B. Ants have many types of nests.
C. Ants are social insects.
D. Ants are smart insects.

Best evidence sentence: **1**

5. List the three main jobs of the queen ant. (supporting details)
1. She finds a place to nest. 2. She lays her eggs. 3. She cares for all the baby ants.

Best evidence sentence per job: **16, 17, 18**

6. From reading the passage, you could say that ants are: (character trait, inference)
A. hard working.
B. lazy.
C. strong.
D. not helpful.

2 best evidence paragraphs: **C, D**

45. A Skateboarder Speaks Out (p. 124)
Reading Level: 3.5

1. Where did the action of the story take place? (setting)
on the city beach trail near the ocean.

2 best evidence sentences: **1, 2**

2. What caused Cam to keep her speed down on the trail? (cause/effect)

She didn't want to run into anybody.

Best evidence sentence: **4**

3. Why was Cam surprised when the police officer stopped her? (inference)
   A. She was keeping her speed down.
   B. She had already been stopped earlier.
   C. She didn't see the policeman coming.
   D. She had been passed by people on rollerblades.

Best evidence sentence: **4**

4. Put the following events in the order they actually happened. (sequence)
   4 Cam writes the letter.
   2 Bikers pass Cam on the trail. (6)
   1 Cam decides to ride her board on the trail. (1)
   3 The policeman stops Cam. (7)

5. Using paragraphs C and D, give two reasons why Cam feels skateboarding should be allowed on the city beach trail. (supporting detail) Accept any 2:
   You can ride a bike on the trail (13).
   You can rollerblade on the trail (14).
   Your dog is allowed on the trail (15).
   It's unfair (17). **Most skateboarders know how to control their boards** (24).

Best evidence: **13, 14, 15, 17, 24**

6. What is the main idea of the letter? (main idea)
   A. Cam thinks everyone should ride skateboards.
   B. Cam tells her story to get support for her opinion.
   C. Cam thinks rollerblading should be against the law.
   D. Cam explains the problem she had on the city trail.

B is the best answer because Cam is trying to persuade the city council that skateboarding should be allowed on the beach trail. There is no evidence to support A or C. Cam does more than just explain the problem she had on the beach trail, so D is incorrect.

46. A Mystery in Time (p. 126)
Reading Level: 3.6

1. Paragraph B mentions a mystery. What is the mystery? (inference)

Strange objects were appearing on the space station.

Best evidence sentence: **1**

2. You could say that Varga is: (character traits)
   A. caring.
   B. selfish.
   C. gentle.
   D. frightened.

Best evidence paragraph: **H**

In paragraph H, Varga yells at a man for bringing no gifts. She makes his cane disappear so that he falls over. Her behavior supports B, not A or C. There is no evidence for D.

3. Sentence 20 shows the narrator has figured out the mystery. Which was probably NOT a clue to the solution? (inference)
   A. information found in Varga's room
   B. the fact that a zapper was missing
   C. his dressing for the year 1232
   D. the setting on the time machine

Choice C is a result of sentence 20. The other 3 choices are events that occur before sentence 20 and are clues to his figuring out the mystery.

4. The story takes place in two different settings. Give one of them. (setting)

A space station. **A castle on Earth** (Also acceptable: **The throne room of a castle on Earth**)

5. Match each cause with its effect. Fill in each blank with the letter of the correct cause. (Causes are lettered A–D, results are listed below them.) (cause/effect)
A. The wagon ride is bumpy.
B. The station zaps her.
C. Varga zaps the cane.
D. The man brings no gifts.
D Varga zaps the cane.
A The seat shakes hard.
C The man falls down.
B Varga disappears from the throne.

6. Predict what the narrator might find back at the station.

Varga (Also acceptable: **The objects are gone** [they were returned to the castle])

Sentence 35 suggests the narrator told the station where Varga was; then she disappeared. Sentence 39 suggests the objects went back to the castle.

7. There was conflict between: (conflict)
A. Varga and the old man.
B. the people on the station.
C. the narrator and the old man.
D. the narrator and the time machine.
Best evidence paragraph: **H**

In sentence 28, the man says he has no gifts. Varga then growls at him and zaps his cane in paragraph H. There is no evidence for choices B, C, or D.

47. Island Patriot (p. 128)
Reading Level: 3.8

1. Number the events from paragraphs B and C in the order they really happened. The first one has been done for you. (sequence)
2 Most Patriots give up. (13)
4 Johnston sees a ship with his spyglass. (5, 7)
3 Johnston attacks the *Sir Robert Peel*. (15)
1 Patriots are beaten in Toronto. (12)

2. As used in sentences 3 and 22, the word *maze* probably means: (vocabulary)
A. system of pathways where it's easy to get lost.
B. open waters where you can move quickly.
C. border of three countries.
D. amazing area for sightseeing.
Best context clue from paragraph D: **23**

3. Johnston attacked British ships because he wanted to: (cause/effect)
A. find more money.
B. get back at Canadians.
C. get attention.
D. make the British leave.
Best evidence sentence: **24**

4. The setting of the story is: (setting)
A. a river between Canada and the U.S.
B. islands between the U.S. and Britain.
C. the Canadian bushlands.
D. the British Isles.
2 best evidence sentences from paragraph A: **2, 4**

5. Which is NOT true of the Thousand Islands? (inference)
A. It is in the St. Lawrence River.
B. It lies between Canada and the U.S.
C. It could be called a maze of waterways.
D. It contains the city of Toronto.
All choices but D can be proven true by information in the passage. A is true by sentence 2, B by sentence 4, and C by sentence 3.

6. In what year did the Patriots try to take over the city hall in Toronto? (conclusion)
1837
2 best evidence sentences: **1, 11**

7. Mark each of the following as T for True or F for False. (inference)

F All Canadians were upset by British rule.

T Canadians fighting against British rule were called Patriots.

Best evidence for both answers: **10**

We can tell by sentence 10 that not all Canadians were against British rule. In paragraph B, the narrator (Bill Johnston) talks about showing the British who's boss. In sentence 10, he refers to himself and others like him as "Patriots."

48. Meteors (p. 130)
Reading Level: 4.1

1. What is the main idea of paragraph A? (main idea)
   A. Scientists call meteors shooting stars.
   B. Meteors can be bigger than a school bus or as small as dust.
   C. Shooting stars are not meteors.
   D. Meteors are pieces of rock and metal that fall into our sky.

   Choice D sums up the main idea of paragraph A. A is incorrect. B and C are details within the paragraph.

2. Would city lights make it harder for you to see meteors? Use paragraph B to explain your answer. (inference, prediction)

   Yes. The night sky would not be as dark, so the white trails of the meteors would be harder to see.

   Best evidence sentence: **8**

3. What causes most meteors to burn up? (cause/effect)
   A. high speed and heat
   B. the passing of a comet
   C. dust and heat from the sun
   D. the fall from space
   Best evidence sentence: **10**

4. In paragraph C, what can result from a passing comet? (cause/effect)

   a meteor shower

   Best evidence sentence: **15**

5. The story suggests that meteors are different sizes. (supporting details)
   2 best evidence sentences: **4, 5**

49. A Long Distance Adventure (p. 132)
Reading Level: 4.0

1. What is the most likely meaning of *din*, as used in sentence 7? (vocabulary)
   A. telephone ringing
   B. loud noise
   C. tall buildings
   D. long distance
   Best context clue: **6**

   B is supported by sentence 6, which says it was noisy. Sentence 7 says she could not make herself heard. A, C, and D do not make sense in the context of the story.

2. Kyoko's actions in paragraph C can best be described as: (character trait)
   A. tricky.
   B. brave.
   C. selfish.
   D. mistaken.

   B is correct because Kyoko jumped out into traffic to rescue the boy. This was a brave action. C is incorrect because she put herself in danger to save someone else. There is no evidence for A or D.

3. What made Kyoko disappear? (cause/effect)
   A. dialing the phone
   B. talking to Lisa
   C. chasing a cat
   D. meeting the mayor
   2 best evidence sentences from paragraph D: **20, 22**

   Sentence 20 says she dialed her parent's number; sentence 22 says after a flash of light, she was home.

4a. Why did Kyoko grab the boy's hand and drag him back onto the sidewalk? (inference)

She didn't want him to get hit by the truck.

4b. Circle the group of sentences that best supports your answer.

1–4   5–9   (10–13)

In sentence 10, Kyoko yells, "Look out!" Sentence 11 says a big truck sped by. Sentence 12 says that the cat made it across. Sentence 13 says the boy "would not have been so lucky."

5. What would Kyoko's parents probably say if she told them the girl in the photo was her? (prediction)

They probably wouldn't believe her.

Best sentence from paragraph E: **26**

Sentence 26 explains that Kyoko's parents believe she makes up too many stories, so they will not likely believe she was transported to New York City via the phone.

6. Which of the following are the two places where the action takes place? (setting)
   A. Kyoko's house and Lisa's house
   B. Lisa's house and New York City
   C. New York City and Kyoko's house
   D. Kyoko's house and the mayor's house

2 best evidence sentences: **4, 5**

C is correct because sentence 2 says Kyoko was in her living room, then in New York City. The story has no evidence for A, B, or D.

7. What is the main idea of paragraph C? (main idea)
   A. A cat darts out into traffic.
   B. A boy runs after the cat.
   C. Kyoko grabs the boy's hand.

D. Kyoko rescues the boy.

D is correct because it describes the main action in the paragraph. A, B, and C are details.

50. **Masai Culture** (p. 134)
Reading Level: 4.2

1. What is the main idea of the article? (main idea)
   A. The Masai spend a lot of time caring for their cows.
   B. The Masai's way of living centers around their cows.
   C. The warrior celebration is very important.
   D. The Masai are respected because they have held onto their old ways.

Best evidence sentence: **2**

2. What causes the Masai to move to new land? (cause/effect)

They move when the cows have eaten all the grass.

Best evidence sentence: **11**

3. What is done with the cow's blood when a boy becomes a warrior? (sequence)

It is mixed with milk and drunk during a special meal.

Best evidence sentence: **22**

4. Which sentences in paragraph B support the main idea that caring for cows takes a lot of time? (supporting details)
   A. 4, 5
   B. 9, 10
   C. 14, 17
   D. 3, 4

Sentences 4 and 5 illustrate that caring for the cattle takes a lot of time. B does not support the main idea. The sentences listed in C are not part of paragraph B. Sentence 3 is the main idea, so D is incorrect.

51. **Seven Kisses in a Row** (p. 136)
Reading Level: 3.1

1. Who is the main character in the story? (character)
   A. Wayne
   B. Zachary
   C. Emma
   D. Noah

2. The story suggests that Emma's room is: (inference)
   A. tidy.
   B. messy.
   C. empty.
   D. bright.
   3 best evidence sentences: **3, 23, 26** (or **27**)

3. Why is Emma going to sleep in the tent? (cause/effect)
   A. She wants to get away from the night rumbles.
   B. She loves sleeping in the tent.
   C. She is afraid of the bugs and grubs.
   D. She is camping with her friend Noah.
   Best evidence sentences: **5**

   The tent has fewer places for the night rumbles to hide.

4. Write the number of the sentence that describes the night rumbles. (reading for detail)
   Sentence **10**

5. Which of the following does Emma conclude?
   A. The tent has bugs.
   B. The tent is more fun.
   C. The tent is safer.
   D. The tent is in the back yard.
   Best evidence sentence: **23**

52. *Chocolate Fever* (Excerpt) (p. 138)
Reading Level: 3.6

1. Why did Dr. Fargo swab the brown spot? (inference)
   He wanted to find out about the spots.

   Best evidence paragraph: **A** (Also acceptable: **H**)

2. What caused Henry to say "Ouch"? (cause/effect)
   He thought it would hurt when the doctor swabbed his arm.

   Best evidence sentence: **8**

3. Which of the following actions supports the idea that Dr. Fargo was eager to learn the results? (supporting details, character)
   A. He sent the swab to the lab right away.
   B. He smelled a candy bar.
   C. He put the swab in a glass jar.
   D. His nose twitched as he smelled the air.
   Best evidence sentence: **11**

4. What was Dr. Fargo really smelling when he smelled a candy bar? (inference)
   He was smelling Henry.

   Sentence **31**

   The brown spots on Henry's body were pure chocolate.

5. Which of the following words means almost the same as *bounded* in sentence 20? (vocabulary)
   A. grabbed
   B. tied
   C. leaped
   D. walked

   Since Dr. Fargo was in a hurry to answer the phone, C is a better choice than D. Neither A nor B makes sense in the context.

6. What is the main idea of the story? (main idea)
   A. Henry smells like a candy bar.
   B. Dr. Fargo finds out Henry's spots are chocolate.
   C. The assistants are surprised at the test results.
   D. Dr. Fargo tests Henry's spots.

   The whole focus of the passage is on finding out what Henry's spots are. Choices A, C, and D are details that support the main idea.

POSTTESTS _____

Grandfather's Medal   (p. 140)
Reading Level: 3.8

1. Why did Ramon take the medal from home? (cause/effect)

   He wanted to show it to his friend.

   Best evidence sentence: **2**

2. Which of the following class rules does Ramon break? (inference)
   A. Wait your turn to talk.
   B. Pay attention in class.
   C. Be polite to others.
   D. Be on time.

   Best evidence paragraph: **E**

3. What is Ramon's conflict in paragraphs G and H? (plot)

   Ramon cannot get the medal because it is locked in the desk. If he doesn't get the medal, he will let his father down.

4. How does Ramon solve his conflict? (plot)

   He decides to break into the teacher's desk.

5. Which of the following is the best moral for the story? (theme)
   A. Family is more important than friends.
   B. It is okay to take something if it really belongs to you.
   C. It is important to pay attention in school.
   D. It is important to think before you act.

   Ramon uses poor judgment when he takes his grandfather's medal without permission. Ramon uses poor judgment again when he tries to get the medal back by breaking into the teacher's desk. C does not apply to Ramon's taking the medal or breaking into the desk. There is no evidence for choices B or A.

6. Which two actions below support the idea that Ramon doesn't think things through? (character traits)
   A. He broke into the teacher's desk drawer.
   B. He showed the medal to Juan.
   C. He handed the medal to Mrs. Ortiz.
   D. He took his grandfather's medal.

7. Which words mean almost the same as *get distracted* in sentence 10? (vocabulary)
   A. follow the rules
   B. go to sleep
   C. get ready
   D. not pay attention

   Best evidence sentence: **13**

   Sentence 10 tells us that the teacher doesn't want Ramon to do this again, so he has already done it before. Sentence 13 supports that he broke the rule about paying attention, so D is the best choice given the context. A is incorrect because it is the opposite of what Mrs. Ortiz wants. There is no evidence for B or C.

8. How do you predict Ramon's father will react? (prediction)

He will be upset with Ramon for taking the medal.

2 best evidence sentences: **26, 34**

Track and Field (p. 144)
Reading Level: 4.5

1. Which of the running races requires speed and endurance? (supporting details)

the marathon

Best evidence sentence: **6**

2a. Which of the following words could replace the word *endurance* in sentence 6? (vocabulary)
A. speed
B. ability to last
C. ability to jump
D. height

Sentence 6 supports that a marathon runner must be able to last the race. Since the first part of the sentence already says a runner needs speed, endurance means something else and choice A is incorrect. There is no evidence for C or D.

2b. Which part of sentence 6 gives the best context clue?

in order to finish the full twenty-six miles

3. What might happen if a runner misses the baton? (prediction)

His team will not win the race.

(Also acceptable: **He will have to go back to get it.**)

Best evidence sentence: **11**

The team's baton must be carried across the finish line.

4. In sentence 7, why is the relay race unlike most events? (conclusion)

The relay has teams of runners instead of single runners.

Best sentence from paragraph A: **2**

5. What is the main idea of the article?
A. Track and field is a sport that includes many different events.
B. Track and field includes several running events.
C. The discus throw and the javelin toss are two track and field events.
D. Jumping includes the high jump, the long jump, and the triple jump.

The main idea of the article is given in the first sentence of the first paragraph. The other three choices are details that support the main idea.

6. The javelin is tossed from a runway because: (cause/effect)
A. it is thrown from a running start.
B. it is thrown a short distance.
C. it must be thrown from a circle.
D. it is used for hunting.

Best evidence sentence: **25**

7. What does paragraph B suggest about the last runner in a relay race? (inference)
A. He runs the whole race.
B. He passes the baton many times.
C. He races against his own team.
D. He never passes the baton.

Best evidence sentence: **11**

GLOSSARY OF TERMS

character trait: tells what a person is like, such as greedy or kind

conclusion: a decision the reader makes based on evidence given in the story

conflict: a problem between two characters, or between a character and some other force, such as nature. Sometimes a character has an inner conflict where he or she must make a choice.

context: the other words in a sentence that help give meaning to an unknown word

fable: a very short story that teaches a moral

inference: a conclusion that is suggested by the evidence in a story, but not directly stated

narrator: the person or character who is telling the story

outcome: the ending or result

plot: the structure of the events in a story. Most plots begin with a problem or conflict that builds to a high point and is then resolved.

point of view: how a character or narrator feels about what happens in a story

resolution: the solving of the problem or conflict in a story

sequence: the order in which the events of the story happen

setting: the time and place a story happens

summary: a brief review of the plot of a story

theme: the underlying meaning of the story. The truth that is proven by the story.

topic: the subject of a story or article

LITERATURE CITATIONS

The Barn
From THE BARN by Avi. Copyright © 1994 by Avi. Reprinted by permission of Orchard Books, New York. All rights reserved.

Sable
From SABLE by Karen Hesse. Copyright © 1994 by Karen Hesse. Reprinted by permission of Henry Holt and Company, LLC.

Dexter
From DEXTER by Clyde Robert Bulla. Copyright © 1973 by Clyde Robert Bulla. Thomas Y. Crowell Company, New York.

The Cricket in Times Square
Excerpt from "Harry Cat" from THE CRICKET IN TIMES SQUARE by George Selden, illustrated by Garth Williams. Copyright © 1960 by George Selden Thompson and Garth Williams. Reprinted by permission of Farrar, Straus and Giroux, LLC.

The Stories Huey Tells
From THE STORIES HUEY TELLS by Ann Cameron. Copyright © 1995 by Ann Cameron. Reprinted by permission of Alfred A. Knopf Children's Books, a division of Random House, Inc.

Sideways Stories From Wayside School
Copyright © 1978 by Louis Sachar. Used by permission of HarperCollins Publishers.

Seven Kisses in a Row
Copyright © 1983 by Patricia McLachlan. Used by permission of HarperCollins Publishers.

Chocolate Fever
"Calling Dr. Fargo," from CHOCOLATE FEVER by Robert Kimmel Smith, copyright © 1972 by Robert Kimmel Smith. Used by permission of G.P. Putnam's Sons, a division of Penguin Putnam Inc.